Corporate Games

Outthink the Competition and Take It All

By Michelle Edith Jones

Corporate Games

Outthink the Competition and Take It All

Michelle Edith Jones

B.I.C. BOOK PUBLICATIONS

INK ARRANGED FOR YOUR ENTERTAINMENT

Chicago, Illinois

A lot of levity and artistic license has been injected into this book, but I assure you that I'm not just trying to be funny. I'm trying to be provocative—to startle you into rethinking how you view job interviews, advancement, and the obstacles (human or otherwise) blocking you from reaching your career goals. I'm sharing my experiences (good and bad) with you in the hope that you can either learn from my mistakes or readily recognize your own when you make them and recover from them quickly. Over the years, I've helped many friends get the jobs they wanted. This book is my attempt to reach a wider audience, give you something to think about, and possibly help you in the process.

This publication, although it offers advice to those currently seeking corporate jobs, is not the "Bible" of corporate employment, and it should be understood that the reading of this book will in no way guarantee anyone a job. This book is a mash-up of corporate tell-all, memoir, and commonsense self-help meant to entertain and inform. While I hope to help you, not every trick will work for everybody. Any benefits you receive in regard to gainful employment from reading this book will be a most happy coincidence.

Library of Congress Control Number: 2013944317
B I C Book Publications, Chicago, IL

BACK COVER CREDITS
Photography by J. Novakovic | Bauwerks, Inc.
Makeup by Krystyn Johnson | Chicago Makeup Artist
Hair by: A. Habibu | Leru African Hair Braiding

Local Talent in Chicago, Illinois

Acknowledgements

I would like to thank my aunt Carolyn Maria Fields (April 7, 1943–February 9, 2013) for wanting to help me (and to get herself a three-hundred-dollar referral fee in the process) so much that she badgered me about applying for an office job at a major corporation in Chicago until I did. It was her determination, and not my own desire, that began my ascent of the corporate ladder. Without her pushing me along, God only knows where I'd be today. ("Do you want fries with that shake? Thank you, and please come again.")

I'd also like to thank my father, Robert M. Jones, and my sister, Janis M. Ivory, for believing that I actually could put twenty-five thousand words together into a book that people would want to read. My father gets thanked twice because, once I decided to write a book, he wouldn't let me go a day without working on it. Thanks for nagging me, Dad!

Finally I'd like to thank my cousin David W. Jones, who voluntarily read my rough draft from first page to last and did a great job of correcting my errors without discouraging me from trying to publish my first book. If you had seen the original copy, you'd know what a miracle worker he really is.

Contents

Introduction

Whether you find yourself considering taking an office job at a corporation for the first time in your life or you're working in such a position already, this book can help you with your journey up the corporate ladder. It's a trip I started more than twenty years ago, and I wish I had been in possession of a guide like this one. Some pointers would have made the climb a shorter and easier trip.

No matter what position you intend to hold, always remember that corporate employment is as competitive as a soccer match between archrivals. But instead of achieving goals as a team, it's every player for himself. The old corporate adage is "There's no *I* in team." But if you look closely, you'll find that there is a *me* in team as well as a fitting anagram that defines our whole American employment structure: *meat*. Competition for jobs, promotions, titles, money, benefits, and accolades is fierce. You don't have to do anything unscrupulous to succeed in business, but at times the line between good and downright evil is blurred. Few people have the stomach for competition at these levels. But if you think you do, I'm here to help you.

Even if you have no desire for advancement and just want to keep the job you currently have, you should read this book because, chances are, there are ambitious people out there who are after your job, and this book will help you see them coming and stop them from taking you out of the game.

Who should read this book? Anyone interested in an office job of any kind at a large company should read this book. Anyone who's over the age of eighteen and under the age of retirement should read this book. Ambitious people should read this book. Lazy people who want to protect their jobs from corporate predators should read this book. Anyone and everyone who can read English—whether as a first or second language—should read this book.

I clawed my way up from temporary records clerk to business analyst with only a high school diploma and a fierce competitive streak as credentials. If you're half as ambitious as I am, trust me, you can do the same thing.

Chapter 1

A Bit of History

Riverside Plaza, Chicago, IL • M.E. Jones

I looked at this scene every business day for approximately five years before the company I worked for, Hanover Insurance Company, moved to an office park called the Chancellory in Itasca, Illinois.

The white building on the left is 222 South Riverside Plaza. Chicago's Union Station is housed beneath it, and my path toward a business career began on the building's sixteenth floor.

In 1984 I moved to Chicago, Illinois, from Denver, Colorado, where I had lived for a little over a year. During that time I had a variety of jobs. I was a maid, a dishwasher, a newspaper ad inserter, a display maker, a nurse aide, a construction worker, a linen factory worker, a weigh master, and a day laborer for hire. The reason for all these different forms of employment wasn't just because I was young and undecided about a career path. It was because at twenty-two I was considered an adult and was alone in a strange city and needed to do whatever it took to support myself with minimal skills and education. At that age I was still extremely immature and lacked the patience and temperament required to succeed long-term at menial labor. Additionally I had no real skills to speak of, my highest level of education was high school, and the only jobs readily available to people like me were in the fast food industry.

Please don't think I'm knocking the fast food industry as a source of employment, because I'm not. I was raised on Big Macs, Sliders, and Whoppers like many other Americans who grew up during the 70s and 80s, and I have a healthy appreciation for people who work at restaurants. I commend anyone who has the patience to serve food to hungry, often unruly, American patrons. Fast food establishments provide a necessary and welcome service to people on the go or those who can't cook for themselves or their families without poisoning a beloved relative.

As a teen, I never had the pleasure of working at a Burger King, K Fried, Taco Bell or Mickey D's, but for some strange reason, I suffered for years from nightmares about working at such places and severely burning myself trying to operate a fryer. The dreams usually involved images of deep fried hand or foot. Don't ask about the deep fried foot.

So I'm not knocking a temporary or permanent career in fast food. I'm just telling you that from a very early age, the klutzy child who grew up to become this even klutzier adult knew that for my sake—and that of the general public—I needed to stay on the customer side of the fast food counter at all times.

So even though I worked a variety of odd jobs in Denver, my employment opportunities were still limited by my lack of skills and minimal education. Or so I thought.

When I got to Chicago, I couch surfed at the homes of several friends and relatives. The plan was to get a job doing anything and everything and earn enough money to go back to Denver and give life there another go. However, my Aunt Carolyn worked for an insurance company that offered a three-hundred-dollar referral fee, and she wanted me to apply for the temporary job they had available. She considered it a win-win-win situation for all parties concerned. The company needed a file clerk temporarily to replace a worker out on maternity leave. I needed a job. She needed that extra three hundred dollars. But after having attended high school with my baby brother and sister and experiencing firsthand the disadvantages of being in close proximity to blood relatives as I tried to go about daily life,

I developed a rule of never working with or near a relative, and this rule was sacrosanct. I would rather have given her the three hundred dollars (if I'd had it) out of my own pocket than to have broken this rule.

But there was another reason I didn't want the job. Up until that point, the jobs I'd worked had been extremely physical, and the last few had allowed me to spend copious amounts of time outside in the sunlight and fresh air. I wasn't ready to give it up for a steady income earned indoors. (See, still no signs of maturity). I had not yet experienced life as an office worker, but I had the impression that it was the kind of work performed in a very confining environment. Just thinking about it made me feel claustrophobic.

So because my aunt continued to pressure me to complete the application for a job I repeatedly told her I didn't want, I eventually gave in, but I did it *my* way. I didn't want the job, so I did everything I had ever been told not to do when filling out an application: I wrote in pencil and misspelled words (including my own name); I balled it up several times to make it wrinkled; I stated that I did not finish high school or complete a GED; I reported that I had been convicted of a felony—assaulting a coworker with a stapler. On top of all this, I showed up to my interview wearing, of all things, ripped cords, dirty gym shoes, and a Mickey Mouse T-shirt that was also ripped and faded. Aunt Carolyn heard I was in the office and rushed up to the front desk with some of her office friends to see me. Just one look and she was utterly mortified. She rolled her eyes, turned her back on me, and walked away. She pretended not to know me, as her friends asked, "Is *that* your niece?" I'm not sure, but I think the answer was "I don't know who you're talking about."

I was expecting the supervisor I was scheduled to meet with to react in a similar manner, but she was paid to be a professional and somehow managed to conduct the entire interview with a straight face. Perhaps having her boss in the room with us during the meeting was a motivating factor. I know that if I had been in her shoes, I wouldn't have been able to hold back the laughter or disgust. During the interview I slouched, feigned disinterest, and spoke as ghetto as I could. The supervisor for the position concluded the interview by telling me it was a pleasure to meet me, but she didn't think I was the right candidate for the job. She thanked me for my time, wished me well, and extended her right hand to shake mine while extending her left hand to toss my application into a nearby trash can. But her boss, the operations manager, stopped her and told me right then and there that I had the job. The supervisor and I were both dumbfounded. The manager's rationale for his decision was, "She's here. We need someone today. It's temporary. How bad could it be?" He wanted me to go to HR to fill out the necessary paperwork for employment and then to the records department for immediate training. He got up and left the room first. I'm not sure, but I think he chuckled a bit on his way out the door.

So there I was, stuck with a job I didn't want and a supervisor who didn't want me, all because my particular upbringing wouldn't let me turn it down. Other potential employees would have been able to admit they really didn't want the job, or they might have asked for time to think about it and then quietly slipped away, never to be heard from again. But I couldn't do that; my father raised me under a particularly strict set of rules, and one of his rules had been that you take whatever you ask for. Whether it was—food, a job, a favor, or anything else, if you asked for it and got it, you kept it. There was no giving it back. By applying for a job I didn't want and getting an offer—however ludicrous the situation was—I was obligated to accept it and do the very best job I could. It was at such times that I wished I could ignore my parents' teachings, but I couldn't. So I took the job and instantly became as much of a model employee as I could be. I worked as fast, hard, and efficiently as my abilities allowed. On days when the work was particularly hard or I felt underappreciated, even for a file clerk, I just reminded myself that my days there were finite, and I could count them down until the new mom I'd temporarily replaced came back to claim her job.

About six weeks before the job was scheduled to end, however, something had gone terribly wrong. My supervisor and some of her most trusted friends began to whisper a lot in the office, and whenever they walked past me, they would stop talking and throw furtive glances in my direction. At first I was sure they were looking at someone else directly behind me, and I would spin around quickly as if being stalked by a serial killer in a horror film. But there was never anyone there. I started to worry that I'd made some mistake that cost the company a lot of money and even more to fix. I also worried about getting fired. This was a predicament that would negatively affect my chances for finding gainful employment back in Denver. After all, this was still a temporary job. I still planned to return to Colorado when the assignment was over and try a fresh start at becoming a Westerner. I started to ask around, but no one else in the office knew anything beyond the fact that my immediate supervisor was acting squirrelly, even for her.

Four weeks later the whole office knew what was going on. The woman I had replaced didn't want to come back. She wanted to be a stay-at-home mom and spend as much time as possible with her baby girl during her first year of life. My supervisor panicked. She had been counting down the time until I was out of the office, just as I had been. Now she was faced with the real possibility that I'd become a permanent fixture there. She had several conversations with this employee, who'd already given her two weeks' notice but was willing to rescind it for a healthy pay raise. Apparently part of her wanted to be a stay-at-home mom, but a bigger part wanted a larger paycheck. It had all been a ploy (and a good one too) to get more money and benefits. It might have worked had I not been there. Once the operations manager got wind of what was going on, he asked my supervisor if she indeed had received the other woman's resignation in writing, and when she answered yes, it was his decision to accept it and to change my job status from temporary to permanent. And just that fast, she was out of a job, and I had a permanent one.

This was the first lesson I learned about how corporate games are played. An accepted rule is, if you have leverage, you can try to get more money, more benefits, a promotion, or a better title. But the important thing is that you have to know when you have leverage and when you don't. The employee I replaced had leverage up until the moment I temporarily filled her shoes. Had the position remained vacant, or if I'd been a less-than-stellar employee, her demands might have been more positively received. But once I began working at the company, her leverage evaporated like morning dew on a summer day. Had she, as a valued employee, simply returned to work on time after her maternity leave had expired, of course they would have given her job back to her. Because she made demands however, the appeal of having her continue there as an employee quickly wore off.

Corporations are funny that way. The same company that expects a high level of commitment and loyalty from you doesn't always return the favor. Over the years I've seen many employees work themselves into a stupor under the mistaken notion that by doing so they were earning some form of future currency with their present employer, as if brownie points really have an actual cash value. They don't. The truth is these employees were just working at a detrimental and often unsustainable pace for something they'd never get. Such people burn themselves out and are generally the first to be let go in a pinch. Corporations prize loyalty highly, but since they rarely give it in return, I suggest you mold your corporate career around ethics and your own personal ambitions, and leave the concept of loyalty for your relationship between you and the trusted family pet.

Chapter 2

Brace Yourself for Shock and Awe

The second lesson I learned about corporate games is that they're extremely savage. I was trying to be a nice person—everyone's best friend. But I soon would learn that if I wanted to climb the corporate ladder, I'd have to sharpen my claws and wrap my mind around the fact that everything done in the corporate world to achieve success is fair game. In almost every department I worked for, there were role models to show me how not to behave if I planned to be a civilized person, but they also showed me what could be accomplish in business if one could but send her conscience on vacation. Like:

- A supervisor who was allowed to scream at her workers as if she had lost her mind and berate them in any manner she saw fit because her department's production figures were higher than many other departments combined.

- A claims manager who came in weekends and was so dedicated he routinely got bonuses for being a positive corporate role model. The truth was that he was coming in and using corporate resources to obtain his MBA. He had summer interns who were eager to please write his papers for him as he sat in his office watching movies and sometimes porn.

- An underwriter who falsified company documents to cover her mistakes and who routinely lied about instructions she gave to the processing unit. In one case, to cover her own tracks she actually got a processor fired who's only mistake was choosing to help her with her work.

- A VP who came up with a summer intern program so workers' children could gain office experience. Oddly enough, the only children who got spots in the program had mothers or fathers who worked in managerial positions. And the amount these workers made sometimes rivaled the salaries of much more experienced employees.

- A rater who tidied up her desk everyday and who, once a week, neatly packaged up all of her outstanding work in a small box and shipped it out via parcel post—addressed to herself back in the office. She was constantly complimented by her supervisor for being well organized. She would eventually do the work in just enough time to hit her deadlines. When asked where a particular file was, the answer was always that it was in underwriting. Astonishingly, it was years before anyone realized what she was doing, and she was only caught because she miscalculated her return from a vacation and someone else opened her last package.

- An underwriting assistant at a small organization who waited for her boss to leave the office each day before distributing her work to her coworkers with a note that read, "The underwriter requested that you process this work personally." No one ever thought to check the validity of these notes. Unfortunately for her, I was hired at her company to help management "trim the fat," and once I figured out what she was doing, I had no problem recommending her termination.

- A commercial lines manager who scheduled a department meeting looking for suggestions to fix work-flow issues and departmental morale. He later took the best ideas and presented them to his boss at corporate headquarters as his own. He got a promotion, a bonus, and recognition as employee of the month, basically as a reward for stealing other people's suggestions. His excuse? "What does it matter who gets the recognition as long as the changes are made and the department improves?" If it didn't make a difference, why didn't he share the wealth with his workers?

- A pair of supervisors who waited for the head of another department to go on vacation so they could freely poach his best employees in his absence. They invented a mythical yet dire need to fill empty positions in their own department immediately. Their strategy was to circumvent the requirement for these employees to wait to get their manager's approval before applying for these open jobs. And it worked. The two also lied and told the particular employees they were after that they had their supervisor's blessing to go for the jobs. They conveniently neglected to tell two of these workers that, upon his return, their own supervisor was planning to surprise them with hefty bonuses for jobs well done.

- A broker who, while enrolled in a bonus program, habitually screened his coworkers calls (especially when they were at lunch or on vacations) and booked their accounts under his own name. The system was not user-friendly and once an account was booked to a particular broker, changes were difficult if not impossible to make. He stole hundreds of accounts and hit his goals for the bonus program month after month, using OPW—other people's work.

These are some of the milder examples of what people are capable of when they want to further their goals within a company. I can't stress enough how competitive corporate America is. That's why many people, mostly woman, shy away from working in the upper levels of a corporation. The higher you go on the corporate ladder, the more stress you'll feel, as upper managers, the company president, stockholders, regulators, and even corporate clients and customers try to squeeze every ounce of life out of you to fulfill their own needs. It's not unusual for employees working at any level in a corporate environment to develop ulcers, have strokes and heart attacks, or develop problems with drug and alcohol abuse. And even if you manage to avoid these pitfalls, it's hard not to watch it all play out as it happens to the people around you. It's possible for you to develop chronic health problems due to stress by proxy.

This book offers advice to help you acquire the things you want—promotions, prestige, and money—without breaking moral codes. That's not to say that breaking moral codes can't help you climb to the top of the corporate ladder. They can, but the opportunities they create don't last long, and the people in your office will never forget how you got to the top. Some people will still go so far as to try to sleep their way to the top. After I got my second promotion at Hanover, one of the coworkers in my new department wanted to show me something the next Friday night. He was meeting a friend at a nearby hotel, and wanted me to wait with him in the lobby for her arrival. I thought this was a strange request, but since it was a Holiday Inn with a huge lobby, I felt safe. When we got there, he picked up two newspapers, handed me one, and said, "Enjoy the show." I sat down and looked at the paper, wondering what I was supposed to do with it. He held his paper up to his face, and I assumed he was reading it, so I did the same. After about twenty minutes, he nudged my arm and whispered for me to casually peek around the side of the paper at the front desk. Two managers from our office were checking in together. They were married—to other people. I was so startled that I accidentally yanked the whole paper down into my lap, almost tearing it in half. He leaned over and used his wide-open *Chicago Tribune* to shield us. We must have been quite the sight, but I doubt anyone was paying attention to us. I peeked around the paper again and saw the two lovebirds escort each other to the elevator. I couldn't form words at this point, and I just looked at my acquaintance with shock and awe. I wasn't surprised that the couple was having an affair. I just couldn't believe they were dumb enough to pick the hotel closest to the office. I got up to leave, but my companion grabbed my arm and said, "Wait! There's more." And there was much more. I had to leave after two hours. I had learned too much information about too many of my fellow employees. I asked him why he felt the need to bring me here and expose me to this behavior. He shrugged and said, "Because, in a pinch, this stuff is good to know."

That brings up the topic of extorting your way to the top. It's rampant in many companies across America. It's wrong, and I frown upon it. Secrets are the worst kind of leverage to use again a person, because you can never predict how he will behave when his livelihood or his family is threatened. I've never seen anyone actually use extortion to get ahead in the corporate game, but I have talked others out of behaving badly in this way. The stories I've heard about the outcome of office extortion never end well for the extorter or the extorted. Usually both end up fired. The extorted usually can get another job. The extorter is generally the one to develop future employment issues.

Why? Well, because no matter what extorted employees have done (unless it involves child abuse or other major crimes), once they survive the initial embarrassment of having their deepest, darkest secrets brought to light, over time, as the victims in such scenarios, they're forgiven and usually get a second chance. They're seen as foolish, and we can all be guilty of a little foolishness from time to time. So it's easy for coworkers to identify with them and cut them some slack.

But extorters... Well, they've engaged in a crime and tried to ruin other people's lives for profit. It takes a particularly callous type of person to do this. Not many employers or employees want people like this around. Within an industry such as insurance, stories of the exploits at one company will quickly travel throughout the region. It doesn't happen at the actual speed of light, but word of mouth usually happens fast enough to keep problem employees from getting new jobs at one company after another after another.

What about lying? Here I think we've hit a gray area. Sure, I've lied to employers before. I've called in sick to work...from the New York-New York Hotel and Casino in Las Vegas. I've lied about the time it took me to complete a task, because I didn't want my boss to know exactly how quickly (or slowly) I really completed an assignment. I may have told a coworker that a job was more complicated than it really was, or that the position had been filled, to keep her from applying for it. But these are minor examples of what occasionally occurs in an office; I've never lied about a coworker's abilities, and I've only misrepresented my own once. But some people treat the stretching of truth like it's an art form.

I was promoted quickly from a records clerk to a records work leader, a working supervisory position, and this left a vacancy in the records department. A recent college graduate was hired. For the sake of anonymity, let's call her Sabrina. Sabrina had a great personality and a business degree, but something about her struck me as odd. She seemed a bit too young to be a college grad, but I shrugged it off because we needed the help. Within a week she was able to file faster than anyone else, including myself. She became the department's "golden child," and my supervisor started ridiculing me, telling me that I wasn't as good at my job as I thought I was, because here was a new, inexperienced employee who was far better. I tried to work faster and smarter, but I just couldn't keep up with the new kid, and it galled me. I couldn't place my finger on it, but my gut was telling me that things were not as they seemed. I knew something was wrong, but I chalked it up to jealousy and paranoia, and I did my best to push all negative thoughts about this employee out of my mind.

Sabrina seemed to be a phenomenal worker. My supervisor used this woman's outstanding performance to belittle me every chance she could. In fact she was trying to use my new coworker's production numbers to discredit me as the department work leader in order to replace me with Sabrina. Since I was a permanent employee, replacing me would mean a promotion, a demotion, or termination. This supervisor hated me so much that a promotion was out of the question. And as far as I was concerned, so was termination. A fight was definitely brewing in our department.

But my supervisor could have saved herself a lot of future embarrassment if she had just bothered to ask Sabrina what she wanted. Sabrina had lofty plans that only briefly included a stay in the records department. Because she was exceptionally speedy, she was able to finish a complete day's worth of work before noon, leaving her ample time to assist others in our department. But instead of doing that, she spent the time hanging out in the commercial underwriting department. It started with her taking lunch with one of the underwriters a day or two a week, but it quickly became every day. She spent a lot of time in that department, asking questions about underwriting and what it took to become an underwriter. Before long, she was hanging out with the underwriting manager, who soon became one of her biggest fans.

My supervisor wasn't happy about Sabrina's entire salary coming out of the records department's budget when she was spending half her workday in another department she didn't belong in. Sabrina spent twenty hours every week basically earning money to butter up the underwriting manager. This woman was anything but stupid.

One day, I was standing in the office's reception area when Sabrina walked through in the company of an underwriter and the underwriting manager on their way out to lunch together. My supervisor was coming through from another direction and she stopped Sabrina and told her that after lunch, she was expected to come back to records and work in her own department for a change. Or, if she was done with her work, she could help out another clerk. There was plenty of work to go around. The supervisor told her that her vacation in underwriting was over and she needed to focus her attention on her own job in the records department. Sabrina was horrified. She was enjoying herself in the underwriting department and didn't want the party to end like this.

What happened? Well, within corporations there exists a hierarchy based on who brings the most money into a company. Sales people are usually at the top. In insurance, this layer includes the underwriting department and the claims department and they constantly fight with each other for top billing. Underwriters bring the business and the money into the company; claims adjusters investigate losses and keeps the money from going out. The next layer consists of the numbers and money crunchers—actuaries and people from accounting, IT, and human resources. They only fight with each other over bonuses. The bottom layer is made up of the support departments, which include the rating department, receptionists, the mail room, the supply department, and the records department. In a battle between the records department and the underwriting department, the former will always lose, no matter how farfetched the latter's argument is. In a normal world, having one department pay the salary of an employee working in another department would seem ridiculous. But in a corporate environment, things like this happen all the time. It's comparable to the stories you hear about our government paying $100 for a hammer or someone getting charged twenty dollars or more for a single dose of aspirin on a hospital bill. And just when you think you've seen or heard it all... Wham! Something even crazier happens.

My supervisor failed to understand the true dynamics behind the records-underwriting-Sabrina work triangle; otherwise she would never have approached Sabrina while she was with one of the company's head honchos. The underwriting department was a male-dominated unit. Sabrina had been secretly flirting with the men there, and none of them—young, old, engaged, or married—were immune to her charms, including the manager. He listened to my boss and simply replied, "We'll see about that." And then he escorted Sabrina to the most expensive restaurant in the area he could find.

Later that afternoon a huge argument ensued in the commercial lines department. It was underwriting versus records over the custody of Sabrina, and underwriting won. A senior VP arbitrated the "discussion" and determined that the underwriting department could have full custody of Sabrina on a thirty-day trial basis and that during that period, her salary would come from my department's coffers. At the end of the thirty days, if underwriting wanted to keep her, they had to officially hire her and pay her salary from that day forth. Sabrina was given carte blanche to spend all of her time in the underwriting department on the records department's dime.

We rarely saw her after that. Sabrina ran away from our department as quickly as most people shy away from lepers. She spent all of her working moments in the underwriting department. In a strange turn of events, the rest of us clerks had to redistribute her work among ourselves. Normally, we would have been able to hire another records clerk. But on paper, Sabrina still worked for our unit. We had to struggle on, short staffed, for a month. At the end of the thirty days, Sabrina was promoted into the underwriter trainee program, a move that was almost unheard of. She leapt up several rungs on the corporate ladder, skipping the normal progressive stages from records clerk to coder to commercial lines rater to underwriting assistant to underwriter trainee. This move shocked everyone at the company. I found myself in awe of this young woman. No other college graduate had made such a quick employment transition, save those directly recruited into the trainee program from local college campuses, the corporate superstars of tomorrow. Entry into this program was considered to be by invitation only, yet here was a candidate who had managed to crash her way into it. So I began to wonder what a college education could do for me. Sabrina was viewed by many to be superhuman, the stuff of urban legends. Workers in the office anxiously waited to see what the wonder kid would do next as an underwriter.

Thirty days after her promotion, however, she was unceremoniously fired. An e-mail circulated explaining that she was no longer in the company's employ. I didn't know it then, but that is the kind of action companies take when they anticipated a lawsuit. I questioned a friend who worked in the commercial underwriting department and was told that the only thing they could say was that it was due to incompetence. Rumors flew around the office, but even the most farfetched stories were mild compared with the truth. Apparently the college graduate wasn't a college graduate at all. In fact, I doubt she'd ever been near a college campus; she might not have been able to spell *college*. Everything on her résumé—her job experience, educational background, age, and even her references—was false. When she got over to the underwriting department, they didn't immediately realize that she didn't have the business background she claimed to have. It was only after she was promoted into the underwriter trainee program that anyone realized something was wrong. They did some investigating, and it took the human resources department a month to collect enough data to fire her legally. Whenever I think about how much money she was able to lie her way into, I have to laugh. An underwriter trainee's salary back in 1985 was an astronomical amount compared to a records clerk's pay. She managed to collect two checks, which probably covered her expenses for three or four months. She lied her way to the top in ninety days and stayed there for thirty. Had she actually had the credentials she swore she had, her career would have been astounding.

Of course, she not only had been incompetent as an underwriter trainee. She also was incompetent as a records clerk. We found out that, instead of filing the correspondence properly where it belonged, she had been taking unsorted stacks of work and shoving them anywhere she could find space on a shelf. She did a good job of hiding them too. She would wait a few minutes in her assigned aisles and then emerge, claiming to be finished. This left her plenty of free time to schmooze with managers from other, higher-paying, departments. No one had the foresight to consider the possibility that she was lying about her work, and she was able to keep it a secret until the day she was fired. It took us months to correct all the mistakes she made. I don't condone out-and-out deceit of this type in the workplace, but if you can look past the immorality of the situation, you have to marvel at how ingenious her plan was, even though it failed.

The important thing here is what I was able to learn from her. I learned that I needed to start thinking about where I saw myself years from now within this corporation or any corporation. I needed to figure out how I was going to get from point A, where I was, to point B, where I wanted to go next. And I needed to figure out how to do it in a sea of college graduates, who were armed with the tools and opportunities a high school graduate such as myself didn't have. Our fake college graduate showed me that there were promotions to be had for people who wanted to lie their way to the top. I chose to believe that those same opportunities were available for those willing to claw their way there instead, through hard work, determination, and brain power. I didn't realize it at the time, but at that very moment, in the back of my mind, I had decided to go completely medieval on the corporate ladder and chain of command. And it would eventually prove to be the best decision I could ever make.

Chapter 3

Getting an Office Job

The number of unemployed people in the United States as of March 2013 was more than eleven million. That's more than the populations of Chicago, Houston, Los Angeles, Boston, Miami, Philadelphia, and Charlotte combined. Unemployment figures in this country are getting better only because thousands of people are giving up the hope of finding a job, and at that point they stop looking for work. Once their unemployment compensation runs out, they're still a statistic, but a different statistic. Another reason that unemployment figures are falling is that millions of people over the retirement age can no longer afford life without a job, and must now keep their spots in the workforce up until the day they die. The figures may look better, but reality does not.

There is a lot of competition within the workforce. It was once difficult to find a decent-paying job. Today, it's hard to just find a job, period—any job. But it's not an impossible task, and I'm here to help.

This section of the book is dedicated to all the people out there who, for whatever reason, are seeking their first entry-level office job. It doesn't matter if you're trying to break in to the banking, insurance, finance, hospitality, manufacturing, information-technology, or communications field; the first steps outlined in this portion of the book will help you get your foot in the door anywhere you go. Getting a job is like any other process; you just need to understand the necessary steps to get what you want and follow them until you reach your goal.

Chapter 4

The Importance of Having Skills

Not every entry-level office job requires you to have skills, but having them will beef up your résumé. If you're serious about getting an office job, you need to be serious about investing some time and effort into making yourself a desirable employee. I've seen plenty of college graduates who can't use Microsoft Word or Excel properly, and I've met a few who can't even surf the web well. If you can invest a little time to educate yourself on how to use a computer, you'll be doing yourself, and your future employer, a favor. If you have limited computer skills, you first should familiarize yourself with a computer. Although it seems like everyone owns a laptop or an iPad, there are still plenty of people out there who've never had to use a computer for work or for pleasure. Don't be afraid of the computer. As long as you don't throw it or splash it with a beverage, there's little you can do that will break it. If you don't have a computer, go to the nearest public library and use one there. If the library isn't busy, you may be able to get someone there to show you how they work. Learn the parts of a computer. Familiarize yourself with the functions of a computer monitor, keyboard, and mouse. Then when you're ready, learn what the icons (images) on the desktop (main screen) do. Some icons access programs on your computer, and one or two will provide access to the Internet through your service provider or via free Wi-Fi (when you can find it). Try looking up things you're interested in, like recipes, movie times, and sports scores. People learn to surf the net faster when looking up things of personal interest. Once you become comfortable using a computer, expand your searches to include business topics or current events. Throw in a few searches on topics you personally find tedious. Not everything in business will stimulate your brain. Eventually someone will ask you to research a topic that's boring. The better your computer skills are, the easier it will be for you to get through the task of researching dry and uninteresting topics.

If you're using pubic computers that have sound cards in them, make sure you bring some headphones, or learn how to mute the sound until you need it. This is not just because libraries and computer rooms are quiet spaces. It's also because we all have different ideas about what constitutes noise. Your favorite song may not appeal to the people around you, and vice versa. Some people perform better in the presence of background noise, some people need dead silence to concentrate, and others fall somewhere in between.

Once you're ready to learn some of the programs used in an office, you can find free videos on how to use Microsoft Office products on YouTube.com.

Search for Microsoft Word and Microsoft Excel. Try a basic course first, then try the intermediate level, and once you get an office job, go for the advanced level if you think it will be helpful. Also, once you get an office job, find out if your employer needs you to learn Microsoft PowerPoint (for presentations) or Microsoft Access (a database builder).

You should also try to familiarize yourself with Google Docs. It's Google's free web-based version of the Microsoft Office Suite. Documents created or uploaded online can be shared with people all around the world, and this is very helpful when people from different regions of the globe need to collaborate on projects to get them completed. Many employers are adopting the use of Google Docs in daily business, and if you don't know how to access and use it, you really should learn. In order to use these programs, you'll need to create a free Gmail account, but trust me, the time used setting it up will be well spent. If you're familiar with programs like Word, Excel, and PowerPoint, Google Docs won't be much of a challenge for you to learn.

If you're lucky, your employer will see the benefits of helping you improve your computer skills. She may pay for off-site classes or reimburse you for classes you decide to take on your own. Before you get excited, though, you need to find out from your boss exactly how much financial assistance she's willing to give you—if any. Trust me on this. Many people who are new corporate hires hear the words *tuition reimbursement* and *educational assistance programs* and tune out everything else, which usually includes a few very important exceptions. Armed with only half the information, they assume that they'll get all the money they need and that the programs cover every imaginable cost. The truth is they're wrong on both counts. Books may not be covered. Fees may not be covered. You have to get a C grade or higher for reimbursement to kick in. And the courses have to be what your employer considers business-related. That's the important kicker. An accountant wanting to take an accounting class is usually covered. An IT person taking a computer class is usually covered. But records clerks are usually not covered unless they're taking business classes. If you're interested in taking computer classes and need financial assistance, do yourself a favor and make sure your employer is willing to offer it to you before you register for the course, and get the offer details in writing. Not doing so can prove to be a costly mistake later.

Finally, even though you won't be using a typewriter, many companies will test your typing speed before giving you a job. You can purchase a CD on touch-typing at Amazon.com for as little as two dollars. Or you can check the library to see if they have a CD you can borrow for free. Touch typing and ten-key typing are great skills for anyone to have. I myself have very limited typing skills. I can type thirty words a minute using just my index fingers and thumbs. I was really proud of myself until the first time I saw my brother type an e-mail. He borrowed my laptop and typed so fast he popped the poor keyboard loose. I was surprised he didn't generate enough friction to set it on fire. Fortunately for me, my chosen career path doesn't value speed as much as accuracy.

Spend time developing all of these skills, and once you feel comfortable with your level of expertise, list them on your résumé. If anyone asks you where you learned the skills, tell them you learned them through courses offered at the public library. It won't exactly be untrue. If you think that telling an employer your skills were self-taught would make a positive impression, by all means say that during your interview. Just remember that employers differ in their views of the worth of things new and used, homemade and store-bought, self-taught and professionally trained. Sometimes a self-taught skill shows a prospective employer that you're a self-starter, and sometimes it shows them you're unwilling or incapable of making a financial investment in yourself. You can usually tell during the interview process what sort of company you're dealing with from the way its human resources personnel carry themselves. Pay attention to the tone they set in the interview, and you'll be able to figure out what information you should share with them and what information you need to keep to yourself.

Chapter 5

Résumé

The first look at you that a company gets is through your résumé. If you don't know how to create one, go online and search "résumé writing instructions." EHow.com has some easy-to-follow guidelines for résumé building. Search for "10 Steps to a Killer Resume," and an article on About.com will be one of the first ones listed.[1] The suggestions offered here are very good, but the article doesn't teach you about résumé styles or how to arrange content. You can ask your friends if they have résumés and if you can have one as a guideline to create your own. Just remember that you're only copying the style and not the content. Friends don't steal friends' information.

Whenever I hear friends brag about a one-page résumé, I immediately ask for a copy. This version of a résumé is rare, particularly for a person with an extensive job history. When properly formatted, these

---

1 Louise Fletcher, "Is Your Resume Working for You? 10 Steps to a Killer Resume," About.com, http://jobsearch.about.com/cs/resumewriting/a/10steps_2.htm.

one-page wonders are invaluable. There are many different opinions about what page length is proper for a résumé. Some business professionals think you should list every viable skill you have, and the résumé is considered long enough when it's done. Others believe that the maximum length for an effective résumé should be two pages, while still others insist that one page will suffice. The truth is it all depends on the attention span of the person reading it. A well-written résumé will include all of your pertinent data: your education, work history, and skills. It will explain gaps if any exist. Make sure you read through it carefully. But don't just look for typos. Put yourself in the place of the HR person assigned to review your résumé. Based on what you're reading, would you hire you?

There are résumé-writing services, but the only one I ever used produced a résumé that didn't get as much as a nibble of interest in eight months. I didn't even like the format they used to create it, but I kept using it because I thought at least it was professional looking. I had always wanted to use a professional service, but just couldn't justify the cost. This company's services were provided free of charge. I was being laid-off, and at a time in my life when it seemed like everything was falling apart, I felt oddly glamorous having a professional company cater to my résumé needs. I met with a consultant who took my information and would hopeful turn my work experience into a written work of art. But that's not what happened. My résumé contained a lot of corporate jargon that I would never use myself. It was lifeless and had no personality. The real problem with it was that the person it was talking about didn't sound at all like me. It was stuffy and full of catch phrases and fragmented sentences that made absolutely no sense to me. I chucked it, came up with one myself, and had a job within two weeks. There probably are many other services out there that create beautiful résumés, but the costs are usually high.

If you know a friend who writes résumés, ask to see some of her work. Ask her what her rates are and if she can help you. If she decides to create it free of charge, so much the better. I wrote résumés for people in my office for the cost of a few instant lottery tickets or a McDonald's fish sandwich. But most of the time, it was a freely provided service. The insurance industry that I work in is a very small world. It's not uncommon to start a new job and find out you know several people there from an old employer. While it's not unreasonable to be paid the price of a sandwich by someone you're writing a résumé for, unless you seriously contract yourself out as a résumé writer, don't try and make a second living off of your coworkers. You never know when one of them will be able to help you. In the future, when you need assistance, a recommendation, or support on the job of any kind, do you want the person you need help from to be someone you freely helped out, and who thinks fondly of you, or someone you billed because you wanted some extra cash? When it comes to friends and colleagues you care about, whenever you're able, help them out for free. People appreciate it and tend to look out for you whenever they can. It's not like we corporate workers are a band of brothers or anything like that. But we spend just shy of one-third of our adult working lifetime with the people surrounding us in the office, and vice versa. That sort of makes us all part of one huge, extended, dysfunctional family. Cut your pseudo family some slack and kindly help them. For free.

For those of you already in the workforce, it's important to cover gaps in your résumé. In my youth I worked at a construction company in Denver, Colorado, for roughly three months until the owners embezzled all the money and fled the country, owing their staff months of back pay we would never collect. I tried to find work for six months. I managed to support myself with odd jobs, but it was nothing I'd want to list on a résumé. This left a large, questionable gap on my résumé until I realized something. The way the company had been disbanded—documents shredded, bosses off to Bermuda, and a lock out as the reason for losing a job—allowed me to fill in the gap in my résumé any way I wanted. I not only could stretch my length of service by two years but also make up my own job description as I went along. There was no one around to contest my remarks. What did I actually do there? Assistant. What did I say I did there? Office manager. Did I actually use this on my résumé? Yes. Did it help me get a job? Perhaps. It's hard to tell. But one thing I know is that filling that large gap in my employment history sure didn't hurt anything. I don't suggest you do it this way, but instead, if you see the possibility of a gap forming in your work history, legitimately fill it as quickly as you can. You can do this in a variety of ways.

📁 Find a Worthy Cause

You can always decide to fill a period of unemployment with volunteerism. Companies understand that times are hard. It looks better if you can show you've done something worthwhile while unemployed instead of just watching TV at home. You can volunteer at a nonprofit organization or become a docent at your local zoo or museum. Help out at a community garden if there's one near you. Read to children at the library. Or take advantage of one of thousands of other volunteering opportunities. And volunteering does more than just fill employment gaps. It provides you with the opportunity to pick up valuable job skills that other, paying employers want—typing, filing, computer skills, dictation, and transcription—all of these skills and more can be learned at a nonprofit organization and used to add muscle to your résumé.

📁 Go Back to School

Consider taking a class or two at a local community college. This is reasonably inexpensive, and in some cases, you can get financial aid. Take a computer course, an English course, a music course, or anything you're interested in. If it's a class that's part of an associate's degree, you can list that degree on your résumé as "in progress" even if you haven't officially declared a major at your school yet. You technically could take one class a year and list your associate's degree as in progress for about five to ten years. But it starts looking questionable after the third year, since you are, after all, attending a two-year institution. More courses are being offered through online venues, making it easier to take a class without the need to physically attend school. You can submit your assignments over the internet, from your home in a bathrobe in the middle of the night, if you want to. So there's no reason not to take at least one college course.

📔 Help a Loved One

You can tend to an ailing friend or relative and list this period on your résumé for what it is: charitable work. Of course you could lie about doing this, and if you're a convincing actor, you may even get sympathy from the HR person at the company you're applying to. But karma will come back and haunt you for it eventually. Lying about a friend's or relative's health is, in most circles, considered worse than cheating on your taxes. Some people don't do it because of a superstition that if you lie about someone's health, there's a chance that lie will become true. Then it's your fault that Uncle Ned had a stroke or your cousin Nancy was diagnosed with cancer. I'm not a superstitious person of this sort, but still, why risk it? There probably is someone in your family who could legitimately use a helping hand. Just go do it. Cook meals for them, visit with them, or run errands for them. It probably won't take up your whole day, the time you spend with an ailing friend or relative will mean the world to him, and you'll have something to fill that gap with that really matters. There's nothing wrong with telling a prospective employer that you were tending to an ailing individual.

📓 Take Time to Raise Junior

For you parents out there, tell your prospective employer you've been a stay-at-home mother or father. There's nothing wrong with wanting to spend as much time as you possibly can with your children while they're young. Child rearing is considered an occupation. You may not have earned an income, but you were definitely not out of work. But before you get back into the workforce, make sure you're ready to give up your time with junior. Employers understand that parents have obligations to their children, but only to a certain extent. If you start spending the bulk of your workday talking to your sitter or your child's teachers on the phone, your employer may look to replace you with a much less distracted employee.

📓 Get a Temporary Job

For some reason, people tend to forget that there are agencies that can help with job placement services. In fact, most of the jobs available now in Chicago have been placed with an employment agency that's been contracted by a client to fill that job with the best candidate possible. One such agency in Chicago is Aerotek, and they have jobs available from mail room clerks to rocket scientists. As soon as you see a potential gap starting to take shape in your résumé, head for the nearest temp agency and take anything they offer that you can afford to live on. They have office jobs available all over the country. Most assignments are local and pay anywhere from minimum wage to fifteen dollars an hour or more, depending on the work you need to perform. In some cases, you can get six-month independent contractor assignments, if you don't mind traveling. Independent contractors can earn thirty dollars an hour or more depending upon their skill levels. And some jobs come with per diems—an additional daily stipend for room, board, and travel expenses.

📓 Take a Sabbatical

If you have enough savings to last you for a while, you can fill part of the void in your résumé by taking a trip abroad. It's best if you go for a reason other than pleasure, such as research for a dissertation or a summer internship. But having the experience of living outside your country of origin can really impress an employer, even if your job doesn't require you to travel. I applied for school and for a job from a desktop in Saint Lucia while visiting my brother who was a Peace Corp volunteer. I was able to get the airfare at a very low price by booking it well in advance of my travel dates, but my (cheap) exotic travels impressed both my school advisor and my future boss. And the supervisor at the next company I applied to work for after that was impressed that I had just traveled to Mexico City. She would have been more impressed had my grasp of Spanish been better. She got excited at the thought that her prospective employee was bilingual. Nothing could have been further from the truth. Three semesters of Spanish and I can barely order another beer and a bowl of salsa at a restaurant.

🎒 Start Working for Yourself

If you're between jobs right now, ask yourself if you have any skills you can use to generate an income and then get out there and do it. Be honest with yourself. Just because you've never had your own business doesn't mean that you can't operate well as an entrepreneur.

Between my college graduation in 2012 and landing a new insurance job, I was unemployed for six months. I didn't qualify for unemployment, because I had quit my last job so I could take the day courses I needed to complete my degree. I watched what little savings I had drain away. And I began to wonder how I was going to keep going without filing for bankruptcy. I had never had my own business and didn't think I had any skills I could use to make a decent wage. But then a friend, who worked as a trade ally for the utility companies in the Chicago area, wanted my help. He needed to develop client lists, flyers, and postcards and to have mailings sent out about utility products being offered to small business customers. We worked out a fair hourly rate, and I worked for him part-time even after I found a new job. The work he wanted me to do was easily done from my laptop at home. And through him, I was able to find another client who needed my particular skills. I started mapping potential customers for them so their crews had an easier time of finding the businesses they wanted to target. It's a lot of work. In my circle, entrepreneur means independent contractor. As such, I'm responsible for paying my own self-employment taxes on a quarterly basis and keeping track of my business expenses on a daily one. While I was self-employed, I was making enough money to stay afloat; I wasn't making enough money to create benefits for myself. There was no vacation pay and very few frills, except that I was able to slow the financial bleeding that often occurs during unemployment. Now that I am again gainfully employed, the consulting work I do on the side pays for my entertainment, which isn't cheap anymore.

📓 Change the Look of Your Résumé

Finally, you can simply alter the appearance of the dates on your résumé and just show the years of employment, instead of including months and days. Working from December 31, 2012 to February 14, 2013 becomes 2012–2013. You'll have to be prepared to tell the truth about the gaps in your history during the interview, but at least you'll have the opportunity to get one.

But I digress. Let's get back to creating your résumé. After you've chosen a method with which to create the first copy of your résumé, there are still a few steps you need to take before you send it through the mail or post it online. For snail mail résumé correspondence, go to an office supply store and purchase a package of a nice linen paper and matching envelopes. It's expensive, but maybe you can split the cost with others who also need these supplies. Select an off-white or light-gray color, something that will stand out in an endless sea of mail but that won't blind people. And whatever you do, please do not use neon orange for anything, not even as a joke or on a dare.

Review your résumé for typos several times before printing it, because the paper costs too much to waste.

Make sure your résumé is easy to read: keep the length to a page or two, bold your headings, and italicize company names. If you have no job experience but have attended college or a trade school, write a curriculum vitae instead. It should specifically lists courses you've taken that are pertinent to the position you're applying for. While a curriculum vitae generally is used for school applications and grant proposals, if you have no other experience, your completed course list and grades will have to do.

If your handwriting is bad, print envelope labels from a computer, or have someone else address them for you. Once I went around the office asking people for handwriting samples and found a woman whose handwriting was shockingly beautiful. In her spare time, she was an artist and taught calligraphy classes. I asked her to address three envelopes for me. I got interviews for all three jobs, and in one interview, the manager had my envelope in hand. She never asked me about it, but I could tell by the way she held onto it that the calligraphy had made an impression. While it was unfortunate that my own handwriting is more like an unbreakable code, it didn't matter. There's no shame in using every angle at your disposal, including someone else's handwriting, to get your foot in the door.

When it's time to stamp the envelope, don't just use what's on hand. Go to the post office and see what stamps are available. Choose stamps in a classic style, such as the US flag, over cartoon characters. I'm usually still putting Christmas and Kwanzaa postage stamps on my bills in June, but you would never catch me using them to send correspondence to a potential employer.

If you're submitting your résumé online, you'll have to rely on style, readability, and catch phrases. Most résumés submitted online never see a person anymore. They're filtered through a computer program that looks for specific skills and keywords that describe your personality and work ethic. Your résumé might be a graphic artist's dream, but if a computer kicks it out, a living, breathing person will never get the chance to see it. These programs screen your résumé and look for selected keywords to trigger the need for a person to read it. Keywords include specific skills and job-related responsibilities as well as character traits. Some such words are *confident, managed, trained*, and *determined*. On your résumé, mirror some of the terms found on the job boards if they match your skills. The next time you're on a job board like Monster or Careerbuilder, pay close attention to what qualities employers are looking for. They're looking for people who are energetic, organized, detail orientated, independent, and skilled. If any of these words describe you, the real you, by all means work them into your résumé.

There are hundreds of such words, like *facilitate, implemented, achievement*, and *develop*, which can help your résumé get noticed. There are also words and phrases you should avoid because they're so overused that they grate on people's nerves—words such as *team player, problem solver*, and *self-motivated* are meaningless unless you have concrete examples from past experiences you can use to back them up. Just tell your prospective boss what you've done, and let him decide if your past actions merit your getting the job or not.

It's tempting to try to guess what an employer wants to hear and then fill your résumé with catch phrases designed to get attention. Whatever you do, don't become a victim of your own handiwork. Don't lie about skills you don't have. Don't knowingly over-inflate accomplishments that, once on paper, may be researched and disproved by a diligent HR supervisor. Many prospective employees make the mistake of thinking that human resources employees don't check references or job histories. At best, this is wishful thinking. I've been tempted a time or two myself to misrepresent my credentials, just to see if anyone was paying attention. But, except for that first insurance job I had, every position I've applied for was one I really wanted to get. Why would I want to risk losing it by overinflating my skills just to satisfy some freakish bout of curiosity? My advice to you is that you should not describe someone in your résumé that you're not. If you do, you'll be painting yourself into a corner. I once got a job solely based on promises I couldn't keep. I was blinded by the offered salary. I was greedy, and my selfishness soon came back to haunt me. I spent more time frantically trying to learn skills I didn't have than doing the actual job. I entertained my boss, because the stress I was under was of my own design. I was running around in circles and into walls scrambling to keep up with a position

I should never have gotten. I did a poor job, but was able to hang on long enough to transfer somewhere else. I ended up embarrassing myself by focusing too much on the salary and not enough on the job I was being asked to perform.

There are two last notes about your résumé. First, please don't forget to include a section that lists your interests or hobbies. Even in business, people are looking for kindred spirits. It gets lonely at the top. Managers are surrounded by people who will pretend to have shared interests with them in an attempt to get closer to the people they think can positively influence their careers. When a manager reads that someone she's never met shares her interests—cooking, biking, country music, NASCAR—she'll remember this. It's not like you would make this stuff up for someone you don't know. You'd be surprised at how having something in common with a manager can change your life. I once got a job because I listed one of my hobbies: numismatics. There is a simpler term for this hobby, but I purposely used this word because I was testing the knowledge of the person reading my résumé. I was hoping that person would ask me about it during the interview. My future supervisor didn't get it; the HR department manager didn't get it; but an underwriting manager I would eventually work for did, and he shared the same hobby. We were both avid coin collectors, and he couldn't wait to meet me once he found out I shared his hobby. People with common bonds tend to stick together, and it's good to know that you and upper managers have common interests. Who knows? In Chicago it's not unheard of for managers and supervisors to throw extra tickets your way and invite you to sporting events, movies, concerts, and plays once they know you have the same interests as them. This is exactly how I saw my first and only Chicago Bulls game to date.

Secondly, if you have your résumé posted on one of the Internet job boards, pick one day every week and refresh it. You can do this by going into your résumé and changing any character on it, save the résumé, then go back and change that character back. I usually delete the first digit of my address, save my résumé, then immediately go back into it and correct my address. This action makes your résumé look like it's been recently posted, when in actuality it may have been posted for three to six months. It brings your résumé to the top of the pile. In a search for recently posted résumé, yours will pop up on top. And it also throws your résumé up it searches over and over again. The same person may see your résumé three or four times, causing them to experience déjà vu, making them think they need to give your résumé a second look. As you can see, job hunting is all about knowing and using the tricks to get yourself noticed.

Chapter 6
Do Some Research

Once you submit your résumé, start researching that company as soon as you can. Try to find obscure tidbits about the company, its employees, and its history. Did you know that there's a book about the history of State Farm Insurance Company? It's called *The Farmer from Merna*. Think of all the valuable information you could get by reading such a book before your interview. If you have access to a computer, use it to find out what the company is all about. If you can do nothing else, visit their website, and familiarize yourself with its design. Try to understand what products or services they provide, what charities they donate to, whether they have employee sports teams, and what sports they play. Study the company's benefits package. This is important because you can earn points at an interview by not talking about the benefit package. By digging up information on your own, you eliminate the need to discuss it during your interview. Nothing makes more of an impression on a supervisor than someone who is not concerned with whether the company has a dental plan or stock options. You'll be ahead of the pack. You'll already know this stuff and won't be wasting anyone's time on matters that are only important to you. Instead, use the extra time to have an actual conversation with the person interviewing you. Ask about the company's philosophies. Comment that you've noticed the stocks are doing well, and ask if a split is coming up soon. Ask if the company sponsors charity events like the Susan G. Komen Breast Cancer Walk, Toys for Tots, or food drives for the poor. Unless you have multiple job opportunities, don't worry about the benefits. Whatever form they take, they shouldn't be a deal breaker.

Chapter 7

Be Mentally Prepared

Once you've scheduled an interview, make sure you're prepared for it. Preparation goes beyond merely getting a good night's sleep. Plan to get up a little earlier than you need to so you can have a good breakfast and a relaxing cup of tea. Leave a little time in your schedule to relax and to calm yourself. Interviews always make people nervous, and they shouldn't. An interview is your chance to shine as a human being. Just be you. The calmest person who interviews for the job will probably get it. You're not just competing against people you don't know; you're also competing against yourself. You may have heard the expression, "You are your own worst enemy." We muck up great opportunities for ourselves all the time. If you remain calm, you can get through this.

When you get to the office, greet everyone you meet with a firm and genuine handshake. Don't try to rip anyone's arm off, but make it memorable. Smile. There's nothing to be nervous about. They can only say yes or no to hiring you. You won't face a firing squad if they decide you're not the best candidate for their job. Memorize the names of everyone you meet, even the receptionist who greets you. Be prepared to use those names when you leave. It will leave a lasting impression on the interviewer.

Usually the interviewer will take you to a room where the two of you can talk in private. As you walk through the office towards the room, make a comment on something you see, like, "Wow! What a nice view," or, "I've seen that phone system before. Do you like it?" Make some kind of positive comment about the way the office looks. It shows you're paying attention. It can also break the ice and get a smile out of the interviewer. And if that happens, it should be easier for you to relax during the whole process. Calm and cool people get jobs.

During the interview you should stick to the facts. Don't go off on tangents. Assume you have less time than you originally thought to make a good impression, because that's probably true. Most people don't realize that the interviewer forms a first impression of the applicant within thirty to sixty seconds. That doesn't sound like a lot of time, but I assure you, it is. It's an eternity. And that's all the time you need to make a great impression. Don't believe me? In 2012, the Illinois State Lottery hosted a promotion called the Anything's Possible Contest. The rules required you to upload a thirty-second video introducing yourself and explaining why you believe anything's possible. The object was to win $20,000. If you had thirty seconds, what would you say about your life? How much more could you get out beyond your name? To give you an idea of how long thirty seconds is, here's exactly what I said:

> Hi. My name is Michelle, but you can call me MJ. I believe that anything is possible because in December of this year, I will be graduating with a BA and two majors—one in geography and the other in environmental studies—from Northeastern Illinois University at the age of fifty. Honey, if I didn't believe anything and everything is possible, I wouldn't be here today. Thanks a lot, and have a great day.

That's more than enough information about me than anyone needs in a minute, or rather, in twenty-four seconds. If you're nervous about an upcoming interview, take some time to create a calm, orderly thirty-second synopsis of your life. You may surprise yourself with how good it actually sounds. Rehearse it over and over again in your mind. Walk into that interview with a strong sense of who you are. Leave your nerves at the door, and just be yourself.

Tell the interviewer what you can do for the company, being honest about both your qualifications and your flaws. I once interviewed for a job and was told that I might be expected to fill in for the receptionist when she went to lunch, on breaks, or away during vacation. I hate working switchboards. Did I tell the interviewer that? Of course not. Instead I told her *why* I hate switchboards:

To tell you the truth, I've never liked switch-boards. I find most systems are too complicated. But if you're willing to get me the training I'll need, and if you have enough patience, I'll learn it and have no problem performing that task.

By the end of the interview, I was told that if it was up to her, I'd be hired on the spot. It could have gone the other way. I might have ruined my chances by being blunt, but thankfully I didn't. What I did do, though, was put the truth out there. If I was hired and indeed had problems with the phone system later, at least I had warned somebody. This simple act also showed that I knew I wasn't perfect, and I wasn't afraid to admit it and point out my own flaws.

Chapter 8
What You Should Want to Know

There is one question you should always ask about a job you're interviewing for out of self-preservation. You should ask why the job is open. It may be a newly created position that should have been filled by an existing, now disgruntled, employee. Or it may have been filled by a very popular employee who was fired and who left behind a bunch of friends who won't be happy with anyone filling the vacant spot. It might be a job that several people in the company have applied for but failed to get. Trust me—you want to know exactly what you're walking into.

Beware of companies that have had recent layoffs or any type of restructuring that was performed by a reduction in workforce. These companies rarely bounce back without merging with other companies and mergers usually mean further restructuring. The first people to go are usually the newest, unless their salaries are lower than their coworkers'. If you already have a job and are looking to better yourself and your career, steer clear of companies like this, and wait for a better opportunity to come along. If you're unemployed and in need of an influx of cash, take this job and get as much out of the position as you can before it's gone. Pick up skills, take company-offered courses, work overtime if it's offered, and meet as many people in your chosen industry as possible. Brace yourself for the possibility that your newly found position may be short-lived. There are no guarantees of permanence with regards to employment. There never really were.

Aside from why the position is available, you also want to ask the interviewer if it would be possible for you to see the department you're going to join. When I ask this question, I usually get a guided tour of the office, the department, lunchroom, mail room, conference rooms, and more. If you're given such a tour, take full advantage of it. Meet everyone you can. Watch everyone's body language, and look for people who seem to have a problem with you potentially being there. Subtly ask your future supervisor what working relationships these people will have with you. If you won't work together, they pose less of a problem to you than if you'll be sharing a cubicle. At every corporation, there will be people you have to either win over or avoid because they're toxic. It's best to learn who they are and figure out how to deal with them as soon as you can. Also try to use the tour to check out the office logistics. Where will you sit? What does the lunchroom look like? Where are the water fountains, bathrooms, exits, and snack machines? Do they offer free coffee?

If you're not given a tour, see if you can find any information about the department or the company by doing an Internet search. Out of curiosity, I researched a former employer by typing in "employment at [Company X] sucks," and I actually found a site where employees provided candid and anonymous opinions of what they thought about working there. Here is one of the negative comments about the company: "Cons—pay sucks. Doesn't keep up with inflation. No major raises even with promotions." I think this would be important information to know before accepting a job there.

Chapter 9

Stick Around Awhile

The Corporate Trenches • M. E. Jones

**One of millions of cubicles across America, and
your home for five-plus years**

Job jumping, switching from one company to another
in a short period of time, is lucrative but frowned upon.

Although it's a great way to climb the pay scale quickly, its benefits are very short-lived. You can job jump only a few times before companies in the industry get wind of your exploits. As you update your résumé, the behavior that is perceived as your "disloyalty" to previous employers is there for all to see on paper. What employer in his right mind would want to hire you after you've proven longevity isn't your strong suit?

But there's another reason you don't want to job jump. You don't want to leave anything on the table when you leave a job. What I mean is that every skill you can pick up will be of benefit to you in your future endeavors. Skills are just one of the many non-monetary benefits you get from having a job. Other such benefits include networking, professional development and intercultural growth. Trust me, you want to stay in every position you have long enough to use up every perk you can find.

However, job jumping is not entirely unexpected, especially when it occurs in the form of a turnover. Employment turnover is usually high at corporations. This is truer for some departments than others. For instance, the turnover in a company's IT department is usually higher than in its accounting department. This is true for several reasons. IT departments are usually larger and tend to expand more quickly than accounting departments, offering more job openings and room to maneuver. The work in both departments changes through technological developments, but programmers need to be more on top of their games than accountants. IT geeks need to constantly evaluate their skills, learn new languages, and stay abreast of the trendiest innovations in computer sciences.

Accountants, not so much. Once an accountant finds a good paying job, she tends to hang onto it for dear life. IT people go where the languages take them, and they tend to follow the path most likely to lead them to more cash like they're looking for burying treasure. And who can blame them?

Unless a supervisor personally asks you to interview for a new job, or you find out that opportunities rarely come around and you're afraid of missing out, you should keep every job you take for a minimum period of six months to one year. This gives you a lot of time to learn everything there is to learn about that job, maybe even things that others in the same job longer than you never knew, and to develop new skills for your next position. A year is time enough to learn even the fine details about a job, the details that most people don't care about, the details that will set your apart from your coworkers.

Companies tend to have one of three types of training programs—intensive, on-the-job, and self-taught. A company has no greater asset than its employees, yet many corporations cut financial corners and skimp on the cost of training. Intensive training programs focus on a specific professional path—underwriting, claims adjusting, managerial, etc. And they're quite expensive. Employees in these programs are expected to perform well once training is completed, and they usually only have three or four months to prove themselves.

Learning on the job is where you're trained while you work. From day one, you're expected to produce quality work in large quantities, quickly. You train on live accounts and your training program is adjusted not to your learning curve, but to the production figures management wants to hit.

Self-taught training programs are the cheapest way a company can go. It's just you, the work, and a computer system, and you basically train yourself how to do the job. You'd be surprised at the skills you can develop while training yourself. When I got promoted from a mail room clerk to a commercial lines rater, I was in hog heaven. That first day. The trainer came around and put a stack of files on my desk and told me that she'd be right back. I waited patiently for her return, but I never saw her again that day. Or the next. Every other day, I'd run up to her the first thing in the morning and ask her when my training would start. She would tell me to go read the rating course I'd been given and to be patient. She had other, more pressing things at the moment. Well, one week turned into two, then three weeks, and I still hadn't received any training. I finished the rating course and took more advanced self-study courses, but still wasn't confident enough to try working the computer system on my own. One day the trainer walked by my desk and, seeing the stack of work still there, she shrieked, "How long is it going to take you to do this work? When I come back tomorrow, I expect to see some progress."

I was completely taken aback. And I was angry. I had been trying to get her to stop by my desk and give me some training for almost a month. And in that brief moment, I lost it. I grabbed a file, opened up the policy issuance system, and struggled just trying to log on. I had never used a computer before, and I was afraid of it. Just figuring out how to turn it on had been a challenge for me. I entered the policy as best I could and then ran it through validation. I received three pages of errors, most of which didn't appear to be in English. I read through the pages and made changes that appeared to make sense and brought the errors down to two and a half pages. I realized that I could make changes, right or wrong, and those changes would be reflected in the error report as more or fewer errors each time I ran the policy through validation. I made some arbitrary changes, and the number of error pages went up to five. I reverse the changes and the amount of errors went back down to two and a half pages. I then went one error at a time making corrections, running validation and taking notes of what the correct or least wrong answers were. It took hours, but I was finally able to produce a quote. The problem was that, although I was taking notes, I was so angry and scared that I failed to concentrate fully on what I was doing. I didn't write down any decent notes that I could later use to repeat the process with less effort. The second quote was almost like starting from scratch. I made fewer errors, but it still took two hours to enter a simple quote into the computer. This time around I made sure I took carefully worded, legible notes.

With my notes, I was able to go through the stack of policies by the end of the day. The quotes still weren't accurate, but I didn't know that. I assumed that since my work no longer generated an error report, as far as the system was concerned, my work was error free. My trainer came back the next day with a slip of paper that showed the policies I had worked on and the errors that still remained to be fixed. Most of them were cosmetic errors, but a few of them adversely affected the policy premium. The trainer thought that most of the mistakes I made should have been avoided if I had followed procedures correctly. I had to remind her that I hadn't gotten the procedures or any type of training from anyone there. I showed her the original three page error report that I had received and showed her how I was able to correct most of it on my own. It was then that she realized that no one had helped me with the work and that I basically had to train myself to get the work off my desk. She sat down to train me how to do my work correctly and was surprised at how much I was able to teach myself in a day.

From then on, no matter what kind of training program a company offers, if I'm working there, I always treat it as if I need to teach myself the tasks to perform a good job all on my own. I create manuals for myself that provide step-by-step instructions on every job function I'm expected to do. I immerse myself in my new duties and quickly determine the best way for me to do the job. And I don't share the manuals I create unless (a) my boss somehow finds out about them and asks for them or (b) my boss is the one that asked me to create the manual in the first place. And when it becomes apparent that a change of scenery is in order, I make sure before I leave that department or company that I copy every word I've created for my portfolio.

Whatever training program you find yourself in, get as gung-ho about it as you can, and learn the job to the best of your abilities. You never know what's going to happen down the road. A day may come when you need to start your corporate climb over again somewhere else. Every skill you can pick up today will make your transition to another company easier. Not simple, but easier.

Chapter 10

The Hidden Benefits of Entry-Level Positions

Whether you have a GED, a high school diploma, or a college degree, the best place you can begin your journey up the corporate ladder is from the bottom rung in an entry-level position. These jobs are certainly not glamorous or lucrative, but they do hold certain hidden benefits that you should look for and take advantage of whenever you find them. Every corporation has at least one mail room. Most corporations have a records department. The companies that choose not to rely solely on technology to answer their phone calls or route their calls through call centers in Mumbai still employ a receptionist or two. These entry-level positions are not meant to be permanent for anyone, especially for people who are ambitious. They're designed to be stepping-stones to somewhere else within the organization. That's why they're called entry-level positions. It's a starting point. These jobs offer the company a low-risk first look at you and provide your first look at the company. It's low-risk because no one has to invest a lot of time or money in your training.

Even if you have a degree in business or computer science, starting out in one of these entry-level positions may be of benefit to you. They provide income. It may not be considered immediately lucrative, but the salary for positions such as these is considered generous compared to what most people can collect on unemployment. And even unskilled people can sometimes land one of these jobs and earn more than minimum wage. These jobs provide experiences that you won't get if you just stay in your chosen field. And if you have no other job prospects, they'll keep your résumé free of dreaded gaps. As of 08/28/2013, there were 146,678 entry-level positions across America listed on the web job board of Indeed.com. Some of those positions were for medical office clerks, home loan serving agents, word processors, account executives, mechanical assemblers, etc. It's true that these are not all corporate jobs, but it's just an example of the types of opportunities that are out there.

Entry-level positions offer you more exposure to learning materials that will help you understand the functions of your company beyond your chosen field. IT people and underwriters speak two different languages: bits and corporate jargon. It's funny when they get together to solve problems because they really can't understand each other when they speak. Many IT people I've known have benefited from taking rudimentary insurance classes merely to learn the terminology the rest of the company was already using. And those classes allowed them to successfully join in on business conversations occurring outside of IT World.

If you know you want to work for a particular company, but they don't currently have a job open in your chosen department, taking an entry-level position will at least help you get your foot in the door. I knew one man who wanted to become a claims adjuster. I think his brother worked at the company as an adjuster and he wanted to follow in his sibling's footsteps. But when he applied for a job, the only one they had available was in the mail room. He was told that a claims trainee position was coming up in four months, and so he reluctantly took the mail room job. Four months came and went and then another four months and then another. The claims job just wasn't coming his way. But in the process, he developed affection for the supply room. He loved taking inventory, stocking shelves, and placing orders. He said it was like running his own store. Eventually, a claims job became available. But he was no longer interested, because he had done such a good job that he was now being groomed to become the supervisor for the mail and supply unit. His dream of becoming an adjuster like his brother was replaced with the reality of a new career path on a managerial track.

That brings us to another important characteristic of entry-level jobs. Sometime, even for people with degrees in other fields, they offer surprising opportunities for advancement. On occasion, by putting the appropriate amount of effort into these jobs, you may impress the right person and, if interested, find yourself on the fast track to a management position. If you get such an offer, weigh your options before accepting or rejecting a deal. You may have been in the entry-level position for so long that you've forgotten you once had a different dream entirely.

The best benefit to taking an entry-level position is that every corporation has the same entry-level positions. Once you get the skills as a records clerk at one company, you can become a records clerk at another company, as long as your employment history is clean. And you can easily change industries by going from being a records clerk at an insurance company to being one at a law firm, or marketing company, or clinic. The skills you learn are transferable to other companies and industries. Your salary may be lower than anyone else's at your new company, but that would only be due to a lack of industry experience, not from want of skills. However, by starting out in an entry level position, in a pinch, you'll have more options for employment elsewhere than other, specialized workers.

Even if you enjoy working in these particular niches, if you're ambitious, you can't afford to allow yourself to fill positions such as these for more than six months to a year, unless you're angling for the supervisory spot. These are not the only entry-level positions in a corporation. Most departments have what are considered entry-level positions. They're the starting points for particular career paths. There are accounting clerks, IT clerks, processors, trainees, and so on. These entry-level positions are considered more professional that a records or mail room clerk, but in my opinion entry-level is entry-level. Entry-level is where you start, not where you finish. And when you get one of those specialized entry-level positions, you need to advance through them quickly, or you may get stuck in one. I've seen many young accountants come to a corporation seeking a managerial track only to get locked into a low-level accounting job with no-where else to go. They make the mistake of trying to impress people by pleasing them, doing too much, or working too hard instead of showcasing their specific skills and ambitions. They become too valuable where they are for their managers to consider advancing them. Also, in many cases, accountants have to wait until someone else gets out of their way in order to get promoted to a senior position or anything else within the accounting department, and the people who hold the prized positions are rarely willing to give them up without a fight. Most act like they're trying to keep their positions long enough to die on the job. Their day of retirement eligibility comes and goes like any other day of the week. You may not see them for a while, and just when you think there's a new opportunity open for you, they show up for work the next business day, fresh from a long vacation. The same thing holds true for other business personnel: insurance underwriters, IT professionals, actuaries, brokers, and so on. It's usually easier to go from one company's specialized entry-level position to another company's specialized entry-level position than it is to advance within any single department.

That's why I'm glad I started out as a records clerk. From a mail room, records department, or front desk, you can successfully begin to plot where your next career move will take you. If you have a college degree, the people around you will expect you to make a career move. But if you have only a high school diploma, they don't always expect you to have an interest in climbing the corporate ladder, at least not without returning to college and finishing your education first. If you ever run into people who automatically underestimate you, let them, and use their shortsightedness to your advantage. Whether you're challenged to jump into the corporate game, or you just want to find your niche and stay there until you retire, never forget that getting and maintaining a corporate job is all about competition. You've got to compete to get and keep a job. You must learn to look for advantages anywhere and everywhere. A person with a high school diploma may seem outmatched by someone who has a college degree, but what it all boils down to is who can compete the best on paper. A college education is great, and believe me, when you're out there looking for a job, having one really helps. But so does experience, and in lieu of experience, some kind of skills—even rudimentary ones—can count a lot on your résumé. Each of the three entry-level positions previously mentioned offers you tools that will help you start your corporate career. The trick is to know an opportunity when you see one and to take it before someone else does. And also, of most importance, you must learn to practice stealth. You don't want anyone to figure out too early just how ambitious you really are. Ambitious people tend to scare their coworkers, because, like it or not, at a corporation all employees are walking around with big, invisible targets on their backs. You've got to learn to blend in with everyone else, even when you're not like everyone else. Pick an entry-level position, and while performing the functions of your job, use your time wisely. From your low-level vantage point, you can learn everything there is to know about your job, your new company, its major players, what they're into, where you want to go within your organization, and how you're going to get there.

Mail Room

Although I started my business career as a clerk in a records department, my favorite job had to be as a clerk for the same company's mail and supply department. Until every corporation in America finds a way to go 100 percent paperless, this is a job that's here to stay. And it's a simple job. You pick mail up at the post office or wait for the post office to deliver it to you, open it, sort it, and deliver it. You may have to scan the correspondence into a computer if the office is trying to reduce paper. You pick up mail throughout the office and run it through a mail machine that stamps it and seals it. If you work in a small office, you may have to treat mail the old-school way and actually stamp and seal it by hand. Then you bundle it up and take bins of mail to the nearest post office, mail depository, or drop-off location, and unload it there. You also get Express Mail packages together and deposit them with FedEx or UPS. Did I forget anything? Oh, yes, you also read the mail, as time and propriety permit.

If you're employed in a mail room, take advantage of the ability to read. Nothing that comes through the mail room doors is sacred. I was shocked in my first mail and supply position when my boss chastised me for not opening correspondence marked "personal and confidential." I thought that opening anything marked that way was an invasion of privacy. But once my manager explained that people tend to use that designation even for standard business forms because they think it's the only way to get a specific person to look at it, I went tearing through the mail trying to prove him wrong. In the twelve months I worked there, I never once saw anything remotely private. But it did encourage me to read as much as I could.

The information that comes through the mail and supply department of a corporation is limitless. What you're looking for is any information about your company's products, philosophies, customers' likes and dislikes, bills, debts, legal actions, charitable contributions, job opportunities, competitors, sanctions, financials, errors, fraud, cash flow, vendors, complaints, markets, stocks, loss reports, claims, affidavits, and anything else of interest. Without leaving your department, you can amass a wealth of information about every department your company operates. You then can use this information to decide where your interests lie and what direction your career path should take.

Not all corporations are equal, and the information you can get by reading through the daily mail will differ from company to company. My corporate background is in insurance, so as an example, I'll tell you how reading all of the correspondence coming through the mail room was of personal benefit to me. If you're at a different type of company, it will be up to you to determine what to read and how to use the acquired data to your benefit. Just know that the information is there for the picking. And it's free and often enlightening.

🗂 The Power of Periodicals

Another advantage of taking an entry-level mail room position is the periodicals that come into the office. These include magazines, newspapers, catalogs, journals, digests, newsletters and a host of other materials. Keep an eye on the magazines and newspapers that come in the mail, and keep track of the dates they're delivered and to whom. This information will come in handy if you decide to track a particular piece.

Many periodicals will come in simply addressed to the office. Whatever you do, don't read any of them without getting someone's permission. Don't make the mistake I made. I assumed that a magazine or newspaper addressed to my company was the same thing as being addressed to "occupant". How was I supposed to know that the high end furniture catalog that came in to the office was our CEO's favorite catalog? And how was I supposed to know that he had been anxiously waiting for it to come in so he could order a new desk for his office? I borrowed it for a weekend, brought it back the following Monday and didn't hear the end of it for a month. Apparently, I had creased one of the pages. Some people, like my former CEO, are accustomed to being the first or sole person to read a particular periodical (addressed to them or not) and they consider a newspaper or magazine spoiled if someone else gets a chance to read it before they do. While other mail is up for grabs, periodicals have usually been claimed by someone and are considered personal property.

However, this doesn't mean that you never get to read the magazines, catalogs and newspapers that cross your desk. You just have to bide your time and procure them the right way. Periodicals generically addressed to your company will eventually make their way around the office with the help of a routing slip. If your name isn't on that slip, don't get caught with that periodical. Usually a distribution list exists somewhere, and once it's attached to the magazine or paper, that piece of correspondence is routed through the office from person to person in a specific pecking order, and each person initials the distribution ticket once they've finished with the attached periodical. If you want to read one of these, get your name on the list. If you don't mind reading them after they've been through several other people, you'll have no problem.

Periodicals serve two purposes. They provide information to the reader, and they give coworkers with like interests a medium to bond over. The majority of magazines and newspapers that come into a corporation are focused on topics of interest that complement that company's industry. *Forbes*, the *New York Times*, *Newsweek*, and *Money* are just some of the periodicals that can be found near the front desk of many insurance companies. If a periodical comes through the office that has an interesting cover or lists an article you have an interest in, when you deliver it, ask the recipient if you can read it when she's finished with it. Always get the recipient's permission before you crack open a magazine or newspaper you don't own.

Sometimes the person will be so happy to share it with you that she may offer to bring in back issues or other similar items for you to read. Even if you don't think you'd be interested in those other items, don't immediately turn the offer down. Peruse what she brings you, and find at least one article of interest. Study it, and then the next time you see the person who lent it to you, ask her if she read it, and get her feedback on the article. Take some time and talk over what you've read with her. Ask her questions if anything in the article wasn't clear to you or if you want an example of what the article talked about, to develop a better understanding of the topic.

If you read any article and have several questions about it you feel that only the author could answer, ask the author. You can either find that person online or, using snail-mail, you could send a letter to the magazine and ask them how to get in touch with the author. Unless they're totally pompous, authors are usually happy when a reader wants to discuss their work.

The rest of the magazines that arrive at a corporation are for entertainment. Whether it's Avon or it deals with sports, food, music, or gossip there's usually something for everyone. Your job isn't just to deliver it or file it; your job is to see who's reading what. Perhaps you're into golf, and your CEO likes golf too. You now have a way to strike up a friendly conversation with the head of your company, as long as you know enough about golf to speak about it intelligently. Never try to strike up a conversation with someone if your knowledge about the topic is weak, unless you tell her you don't know much about the topic and would like her to explain her fascination with it. People love to talk about themselves, and you should look for ways to give the most influential people at your corporation a chance to do that.

Mail that comes in truly addressed "occupant" is fair game and can be read by anyone who works in the office. These are usually brochures for goods and services. The best use of these is comparative shopping. If your mail room is hooked up with a supply department, take time to learn who the current supply vendors are, who their competition is, and who has the best prices for the goods you need. If you turn up a way for the company to save money on paper clips and staples, let your boss know. Nothing impresses a supervisor more than an employee who can save the company some money.

At one company, I found out that the vendor my company used was one of the most expensive suppliers in the region. I couldn't understand why we weren't using someone else. It turned out that the supplier was the brother-in-law of one of the company's IT supervisors, and this supervisor was in charge of the company's supply ordering system. While his behavior illustrated bad business sense, the only thing he was guilty of here was nepotism. Nepotism happens to be my biggest pet peeve. When I found out what was going on, I started researching that vendor and other vendor's in the area. I gathered data for three months, and then I started ordering catalogs from the more reasonably priced vendors and had them shipped through the mail to the manager of the mail and supply department.

At first, he was confused by the upswing in junk mail. Then I started turning the corners down on items we routinely bought, hoping he would look at the pages and find out how much the company could save on these supplies. He began to take a serious look at the catalogs. Eventually, he was able to convince his boss that they needed to change vendors. They picked up two vendors, one for paper products and the other for everything else. Not only did service improve, but the company saved thousands of dollars annually.

Records Department

If you work for a records department, you'll have access to different information than someone in the mail room, because the files you're in charge of contain memos, emails and worksheets that bypass the mail room altogether. You also have a distinct advantage over someone in the mail room because, for you, whether it's expressed in your job description or not, routine file reviews are a must. It will seem less suspicious if you read a file than if a mail clerk pauses to read correspondence.

During a file review, you can take all the time you need to familiarize yourself with forms, instructions, procedures, losses, accounting facts, and more, all as you're checking to make sure that everything in a file is in the right place. From the first day you start working as a records clerk, you should read every file you can. Files are vaults of information. You can not only find out information about every department at your company but can also read information about your company's customers, vendors, coworkers, and lawyers. If you're lucky, there will be enough information in the files to piece together the work flow in your office. You'll be able to see how the correspondence that comes into the office triggers office activities: file creations, sales, negotiations, litigations, mediations, and agency appointments and terminations. You can even take your time to see how other people get their jobs done. You can learn to use pricing tools, read customer complaints, and see how those complaints are handled. You can sometimes find State Department and federal government criticisms and complaints about errors your company makes as it processes business. There is a lot of information in those files, and it's up to you to determine the best way to put it to good use.

Receptionists

I think one of the most interesting entry-level positions is that of the receptionist. You may not have access to office communications, but if you keep your eyes and ears open while on the job, you'll usually hear the office 411. While the mail and records clerks of the world are getting their information by reading what's available, you'll get all of yours directly from the people you work with. For some reason the people standing out in the reception area of a company tend to forget that the receptionist can hear. As long as you're not leaning over your desk straining to hear what people are talking about, chances are they won't realize that you're actively eavesdropping on their conversation. The office 411 is not the same as gossip.

It's the low-key conversations that managers usually hold behind closed doors to discuss sensitive topics like mergers, layoffs, and office moves. Sometimes these conversations have a way of springing up out in the open, and if you're paying attention, you can become the first non-salaried employee to hear them. How valuable would it be to know that the office was moving to another state in four to five months—without its employees?

While eavesdropping is frowned upon as morally wrong, it's a great source of information as long as you can figure out what's true and what's worthless crap. And sometimes it's the only way to find out what's going on in the office, especially the things that occur "behind the scenes." I eavesdrop on as many conversations as I can. It's like looking for buried treasure. There's all kinds of information out there that people don't and shouldn't write down, like who's having problems in what department, who's trying to sneak a friend into the company in a position that hasn't been posted yet, who's looking for a job somewhere else (and why they're looking in the first place), who's pregnant, or who's going back to school—basically what positions may open up in the near future.

No matter what happens, it's important not to react to what you hear. Don't gasp at bad news, or make uninvited comments, or snort. People should not have expectations of privacy regarding office conversations, even when they're whispering, unless the conversations are happening behind closed doors. Whispering usually invites people to eavesdrop even more than they normally would. People forget that they don't live in bubbles. They'll stop in the hallways, lean in close, and act as though the conversation is somehow strangely soundproofed and protected from prying ears. Or worse.

In the course of my career, I had several supervisors who, while sitting in their cubicles, would start talking about the flaws of a coworker—who sat right on the other side of their partition. Whenever this happens I know I get the strangest look on my face like, "Really? Don't you think you should check to see if Barbie is at her desk *before* you talk about her like that?"

I've overheard my coworkers talk about a lot of inappropriate things, but I never react, because if I do, I lose the ability to eavesdrop on future conversations that can make a difference to me and my job. I'm curious about why coworkers are applying for jobs outside the company, but that's not the kind of information I'm looking for. I want to know about raises, promotions, salary and hiring freezes, overtime opportunities, bonus programs, new positions, and new branch offices. So I've trained myself to ignore the routine conversations people have every day and wait for those rare moments when vital information is callously bantered about the building through the office chatter channels.

I believe you should develop a skill for eavesdropping. This is not to say that you should engage in clandestine corporate espionage—far from it. All I'm suggesting is that you take full advantage of the fact that people love to talk. It's good to be in the know, because even if you can't personally use the information you overhear, maybe someone else can. You can sometimes use the information as a bargaining tool, bartering and trading information with others to get the information that's really important to you. And the trade of information doesn't have to be equal; you can trade gossip for bona fide intel. When I originally wanted to get into the rating department, I had a friend who was already there. I asked her to let me know when a job opening was coming up and to teach me ahead of time some of the things I'd need to know to be good on the job. She, in turn, wanted information about a particularly shy gentleman at the company, including his marital status, dating preferences, and views on marriage and children. And she wanted it gathered covertly. At first I had no problem spying on him, but the more I started to think about it, the more I thought it was just plain rude. Instead of spying on him, I just walked right up to him, told him what was going on, and asked him if he'd mind feeding me some information for my friend. He was flattered that anyone was interested in him and gave me all the details my friend wanted and more. A day or two later, my friend got her information. Two weeks later, I got a brand-new job. Six months later, Mr. Shy Guy got my friend to become his wife. Things rarely turn out this way in an office, but I'm so glad for them that it did.

There's another benefit to being a receptionist that doesn't exist in the mail room or records department, and it involves face time. You're literally the first face anyone sees when he or she comes into your office. This includes not only visitors but also fellow employees, department heads, the branch manager, the CFO, and the CEO. It's important to understand this, because the next logical step for a receptionist, especially one who doesn't have a college degree, is to become an executive assistant. Greeting the CEO every day is the first step to making the necessary good impression required to give you a shot at that job. You can't just show up at work and expect to make an impression. You've got to come in every day and brace yourself for confrontations with people who don't always act their best in the morning. You need to be prepared to balance cheerfulness with efficiency, and try to come up with a way to go above and beyond your job description to impress people in the back of the office from where you are at the front desk. It takes a lot of work, but the effort you put into making this career change is worth it. You'll go from being everyone's assistant to focusing on one person—usually the CEO. I've seen this happen only once, because only one person I met ever wanted this job. If I had known what the perks were, I'd have wanted this job too. Once the receptionist turned into an executive assistant, she laughed herself silly all the way to the bank. She stayed busy, but when she left the office to go to a Bulls game with floor seats, the look of deserved smugness on her face was priceless. Yes, it's hard work. You basically become the CEO's nanny, gofer, confidante, and eyes and ears. You're responsible for making sure the CEO makes meetings and trips, entertains clients well, and stays at the best places the company can reasonably afford. The work is hard, but the perks are rewarding. You can get everything from spare sporting-event and concert tickets to free dinners, lunches, and business trips. And if you care about your job and do the work, you can get bonuses—lots and lots of bonuses. When you become an executive assistant, if your boss isn't doing some of these things to make you happy, keep the job long enough (two to three years) to establish yourself in the role and get the skills you'll need to hit the road and become the executive assistant someplace else.

Chapter 11
All Things Data

No matter what entry-level position you choose, there will be a wealth of information out there for you to sort through, keeping what's relevant and chucking the rest. Whether it's snail mail or memos, get into the habit of looking at almost everything you touch. You don't always have to read correspondence thoroughly to determine if the information is of interest to you. But you should keep a mental list of things to look for. You'll quickly be able to recognize what's important to you and what's not.

If you just do the job you're given by your supervisor, you'll be considered a great employee—for that job. But if you want to advance in your career, you'll need to invest some time and effort in becoming a human information bank. You have to not only know where to look for information but what to look for and how to use it to your advantage.

📖 Learning the Lingo

Are you ready to learn a new language? One of the best ways to use the information you'll pick up in the office is to improve your understanding of your particular company's vernacular—language. Have you ever heard a conversation between computer programmers? Were you able to follow it all when they started talking in bits and bytes? In insurance, we call that *IT Speak*, and since programmers are able to talk to and understand each other, it's considered a language. The same thing holds true for commercial underwriters. Although they speak mostly English, once they start talking about policy coverages, it becomes a mash-up of English and law. And don't let IT people try to talk to underwriters or accountants. That never works. The thing that most corporations desperately need is personnel who can speak more than one corporate language, who can bridge the language barriers of two or more departments. With practice, that person could be you.

Without leaving the mail room or records department, you can broaden your corporate vocabulary just by scanning through the mail and files in your office. In an insurance environment, you can learn IT terms, accounting terms, underwriting terms, legal terms, and claims terms just by reading. You have to find a way to do this without slowing down your efficiency. If you're working three to five days a week, consider keeping a calendar handy and decide which days of the week you want to read what correspondence. Monday could be *claims day*; Tuesday could be *accounting day*, and so on. Or if you have decided what path your career is going to take, say, from mail room to underwriting, familiarize yourself with just that particular correspondence. The more you read, the more you'll know. In a few weeks, you'll be able to use corporate lingo to your advantage.

For instance, when one of the companies I worked for decided to go paperless, I teamed up with an IT technician and together we designed a policy issuance program unlike anything the company had ever considered possible. It produced insurance policies, endorsements, and certificates of insurance with fewer keystrokes and no paper. All insurance documents were burned to CD's, and hand deliver to our agents. And the two of us were able to do this because I knew insurance, she knew Crystal Reports, and we understood each other. Corporate vernacular is extremely important in business and is considered a sign that you're taking your industry seriously. Mail room clerks, records clerks, and receptionists don't need to know how to speak "businessese," but it does make a lasting impression when you can.

Terminology is something you're supposed to be able to pick up on the job. But the records department and mail department are two areas that are, traditionally, black holes when it comes to training outside your normal tasks. You don't have to know a lot of terminology to get those jobs done. And unless a supervisor is sure they can replace you with another warm body, they don't generally help you prepare for promotions. While entry-level is a way into a company, you don't always get a leg up from there.

I once knew a records clerk who wanted to get a promotion out of the department in the worse way imaginable. She tried to apply for every position that came available, but her boss refused to give her consent. The grounds were that she lacked not only experience but polish, of all things. She liked the company a lot but was unhappy in her current job and felt she had a lot more to offer the company as an employee if she was just given a chance. I was already a commercial lines rater and knew she had the potential to become a good rater herself. I listened to her talk. She didn't use any of the business terms that the people around her did, not even the most basic words. I ask her about this and she told me she didn't use any of those words, because she didn't know what any of them meant. That brought me back to when I was a records clerk. I did the very same thing and was treated the same way by my supervisor. The manager of the mail room stopped me one day and told me that if I wanted to get anywhere in insurance, I had to learn the lingo. I did, and it opened doors for me. I now had the opportunity to pay it forward and help a coworker. I gave her the same advice, and with the help of other insurance professionals, I developed a crash course in business terminology called *Name That Term* for her and anyone else who had the same problem. It was a flash card game, and I handed cards out all over the office. I asked some of the underwriting and other business personnel to help quiz her. Whenever she walked by, someone would grab a card and either read the term and ask for a definition or vice versa. It was a lot of fun.

One day the underwriting manager was in the records department. He liked to pick on the women who worked there. It wasn't to be mean or anything. He liked sarcastic people, and the women of the records department could really dish it out. He would ask an insurance question and one of two clerks would usually give him a glib response he considered the joke of the day. On this particular day, he wanted to know what the purpose of insurance was. One response was "to take people's money." Another response was, "to give records clerks something to do with their lives." From down an aisle, a third response was, "to indemnify an insured in the event of a covered loss." The supervisor went down the aisle and asked the woman there more questions, and to each one she had an appropriate business answer. She was then asked what she was doing in the records department, and her answer was that she was never able to get her supervisor's permission to apply for anything else. The underwriting manager promised that the next time would be different. Well, the next position was an underwriting position. But she didn't want it and didn't really qualify for it. So she waited. Eventually, a rating spot opened. She asked to apply, and again her boss turned her down. She moped around the office, and just when she was about to give up the notion of getting out of the records department, her supervisor came up to her and told her that there had been a mistake and she could apply for the job as soon as she was ready to. She was the only one to apply for it. And even though that was never a guarantee of getting a job, she got the job. She learned to speak the lingo and was able to get noticed by the person who could make a professional difference in her life.

"Schmoozeablility"

OK, so you've been at it for a while, and you've read a bunch of information you may not yet understand or know what to do with. The next step is to use it to introduce yourself to people who matter. Let's say you have a piece of correspondence for the accounting department of your company, but you have no idea what the information on it is saying or what value it possesses. When you go deliver the mail or file, find a supervisor or manager in that department to ask about it, but don't just run up to her and start asking questions. You should ask her if she's busy or say, "I know you're probably busy, but I have a question about this correspondence." Why? You need to do this because your interest in the piece of paper in your hand should always be secondary to your need as a mail or records clerk to impress the person who may become your future boss someday. If she is busy, give her the chance to tell you so. She may be busy, but welcome the distraction you offer. She may have a lull in her day and not mind sharing her time with you. Or she may not welcome you at all and view your appearance and question as an intrusion. Whatever the case, it's always good to approach a person in management as if you know she's swamped, hate to bother her, but need to talk to her because she's the only person who could possibly help you. Before you approach her, make sure you have a legitimate question. Don't try to make up something witty on the fly.

Perhaps you've noticed three different versions of a certificate and don't understand the role each one plays. Or a customer wrote in, angry about the misspelling of her name on an address label, and you wanted to bring it to someone's attention. Maybe you noticed that certain forms requiring a signature often are returned unsigned, and you think these instances would be lessened if the original correspondence was sent out with one of those Post-it flags that say, "Sign here." These are legitimate comments that show you're thinking about things that are coming through your department, not just trying to make small talk with a higher-up. It also shows that you see the connection between your department and someone else's. This type of behavior shows initiative and will impress any supervisor looking to infuse his or her department with some new blood.

"Lunch-and-Learn Programs"

Many corporations have no problem insisting that from time to time their employees attend lunch-and-learn seminars that are presented in the office during normal, unpaid lunch hours. Sometimes the company is kind enough to cater the event, but other times these presentations are billed as brown-bag affairs. They can be about anything—new computer or phone systems, new lines of products, etc. They can even be continuing-education business classes. Whatever the case, they work. They're the best way to share new information with a large group of people in an informal setting. And the fact that they're usually mandatory doesn't hurt either. Even if you're told they're not mandatory, don't think there aren't repercussions in store for you at a later date if you choose not to attend. In an office, someone is always watching you. It doesn't look good for your supervisor if she can't get her people to take an interest in the presentations offered by the company. Some are very useful in your daily life, such as sessions on first aid and CPR, investments for beginners, and the basics of corporate operations. Some are mind-bogglingly dry, such as fourth-quarter loss ratio analysis and growth projection through the year 2020. Boring!

But go anyway, even if you find the topic repulsive, because the best data you can collect at a company-sponsored lunch-and-learn program doesn't always come from the presenters—sometimes it comes from the audience. If you pay close attention at these events, you'll be able to figure out key relationships by watching how your coworkers interact with each other. Supervisors tend to sit with the employees they consider either the best in the department or the least annoying. Timid people tend to sit in the back row near the corners of the room. If the people in one particular department spread out, getting as far away from each other as possible, it usually means there's a problem in that department. The problem may be temporary or long-term. When you see something like this, think twice before joining this group. Some people sit with their assistants, and this usually indicates an employee who's down-to-earth and a good person to know. Employees who hang out with people above their pay grade can be either ambitious or sycophantic. Sometimes it's hard to tell until you get to know them.

Lunch-and-learn events are also a great way to mingle, especially if you go to a series of them. At your first meeting, simply observe people, and make mental notes about some of the more interesting or influential members of your organization. Make a list of these people in the order in which you'd like to meet them. At subsequent sessions, pick one person from your list, and, if possible, sit with her or at least within earshot. I'm not suggesting that you eavesdrop on her conversations. I'm advising you to get as close to her as you can and to introduce yourself to her the first chance you get. Don't be intimidated by her entourage, if she has one. Popular people and powerful people are seldom alone. And the people surrounding them aren't always friendly. Don't let them stop you from meeting anyone you think may be of help to you. Sometimes corporate officers get sick of their groupies, and they just want to meet someone to have an honest conversation with. It could be you.

Develop Your Own Strategy

As you're preparing to storm the corporate ladder, consider amending the meaning of a lunch-and-learn program to include whatever information you can pick up in the office by yourself and on your own time. You don't have to give up your lunch every day, but you should consider combining lunch and study at least three times a week. On these days bring in your favorite meal (preferably something that isn't sloppy), and read through the correspondence and files at your disposal. You don't have to confine your studies to dry paperwork. You can strategically pick the brains of the people around you. After a month or two, try striking up a casual conversation with someone in the department you're interested in moving to. Make arrangements to have lunch together at a nearby restaurant, or outside if the weather's nice. Take advantage of the fact that people like to talk about themselves. Learn everything you can about this person—when she started at the company, how she got her job, what she likes and doesn't like about the position and her supervisor, and where she plans to move from here. Her goals may be similar to yours. She may also be further along in the planning process and have ideas that you never thought of. If you're not sure this department will be a good fit for you, offer to help your new friend with her workload either before work, on lunch, or after work so you can check it out for yourself. If she tells you there's nothing you can help with, double check to see if this is really true. She may be forgetting about the little tasks that help make up her workday. When you ask if she needs help, she may immediately think about the big projects she's involved with that can't be performed by people without specialized training. That doesn't really mean there's nothing you can do for her. Find out if her department ever does mailings, or if it has an audit coming up for which specific files need to be pulled, or if there's photocopying or scanning to be done. There's always a menial task that needs to be performed. Volunteer to be the person who does it and, in exchange, ask your new friend to teach you some basic functions of her department when her workload is lighter.

Remember that you need to be doing all of this on your own time, unless you can get your supervisor to agree to loan you out for a few hours each week. Your supervisor will not appreciate you using your department's time to assist another team. But she will be impressed if you use your own time to do it. If she asks why you're interested in volunteering your time in a particular department, don't admit you're interested in joining that department. While this is usually expected, your supervisor won't be happy to find out she may need to replace you soon. Simply say that you saw a need and wanted to help out. As long as you're keeping up with the work in your own department, this shouldn't be a problem.

Chapter 12

Beyond Entry-Level

Before you begin your corporate ascent in earnest, you need to develop an approach, a method of getting from where you are now to where you want to be in the immediate or distant future. In order to do this, you first must take an assessment of your surroundings, paying particular attention to your coworkers. While you work on bettering yourself and your standing at the company, never forget that the people around you will fall into one of two categories: friends or foes. There is no middle category, and more people will fall into the foe category than you think. A person at the company will either be a benefit to you, or she will do her best to get in your way and stomp on your dreams. Although the suggestions for achieving professional growth presented in this book are perfectly acceptable in a corporate environment, this doesn't mean that all of your coworkers will appreciate your ambitiousness. It's important for you to know the kind of people you're working with and whether or not they represent an obstacle on your career path.

Many of the employees around you have found their niches or reached the ceiling for their personal advancement and are content to stay there and leave you alone. Whatever you do, don't bother them unless it's absolutely necessary. These people are like slumbering grizzlies. If left undisturbed, they pose no threat to your ambitions whatsoever. But poke them, and you're in danger of being mauled. They don't like change, not even in miniscule amounts. There's a good chance that these people don't currently hold a job you would want anyway, and even if they do, you should do your best to try to find a way around them to get the advancement you want. When you're measuring up a job that's already filled by someone else and wondering if it would be a good fit for you, stop to ask yourself if the person currently in that spot is a perpetual underachiever, an employee perched on a stepping-stone position, a worker genuinely content with the status quo, or the holder of a dead-end job. It's hard to tell the difference between these situations sometimes, and the last thing you want to do is to snag a bad position from a coworker. If there's another way for you to go up the corporate ladder, take it, and give these people their own space.

Some of your coworkers are just plain haters. Haters come in many varieties. They may be unhappy with their jobs but too lazy to do anything about it, spending most of the day grumbling about the company instead of actually doing any work. They may have been overlooked repeatedly for even the smallest promotion, and now they look at their positions as money they're entitled to due to the longevity of their employment and not due to the effort they put into their jobs—or lack thereof. They may be extremely lazy and do the minimum amount of work needed to collect a check and have so much time on their hands that they spend all their free time and effort backstabbing the people around them. If you observe a coworker behaving in any of these ways, give her a wide berth. On your way up the corporate ladder, you need to practice stealth. Understand that a hater will purposely throw obstacles in your path for no reason other than cheap amusement. Haters are prone to exhibit behavior that is so rude, crude, and socially unacceptable that it leaves you wondering why they still have jobs. At all costs, avoid these people.

Chapter 13

Competition: The Game

From the moment you start working at a corporation, no matter what industry you're in, you have entered the most competitive arena on Earth. Business is all about money: how to get it and how to keep it. Think of working at a corporation like being a contestant on *Survivor: Chicago, New York, Tokyo,* or wherever you happen to live. If you have watched the program, with all its alliances, teambuilding exercises, backstabbing, and devious ways of winning, then you understand exactly what life in an office is all about. There are finite supplies (benefits), and everyone is trying to win the reward challenge (get a bonus or promotion). But instead of having only two tribes, it's everyone for herself. The day you decide to start working at a corporation is the day you need to wrap your mind around being ruthless to get the things you want. Many people shy away from competition. But you can't be squeamish and successful in a corporate world.

This book was originally titled *Stage a Professional Coup: How to Climb the Corporate Ladder One Body—Uh—Rung at a Time*. But it was changed for brevity's sake and because a lot of people disliked it. But I liked it and felt it was appropriate. A career in business is not for the timid. It's a slugfest. In order to make it up the corporate ladder in the first place, you have to get comfortable with climbing over other people and stomping on some of them as you go by. It sounds cruel, but it's true. You'll have to shed some blood—yours or someone else's. Which do you prefer? In business, good guys who play nice rarely finish first or even keep their jobs. Under certain circumstances, such as a hostile buyout or a regulatory takeover for compliance violations, you can grab some popcorn, take a seat, and watch other people cannibalize their coworkers as they fight to keep the few jobs left after downsizing. When things go wrong, people in offices go on witch-hunts, and the motto of the day becomes "duck and cover!" In business, the thing that will really set you apart from your coworkers is a killer instinct and a strong stomach. Figure out why you're trying to climb the corporate ladder in the first place, what your ultimate goal really is, what you're willing to do to reach that goal, and then keep your eye on the prize no matter how deep the muck around you gets. Do you want money? Is there any other point to working? Power? There's nothing wrong with wanting to be top dog. Recognition? You can certainly build a name for yourself as you storm your way up to the top of any corporate tower. You don't have to lie or cheat your way to the top, and honestly, there are much better ways at becoming successful than to stoop to immoral levels. If you want to be successful in a corporate setting, you need to figure out how far you can push your moral code without breaking any boundaries. Push the limits of ethics. Learn to live in the gray areas of industry. Your bosses do. The CEO of your company does. Why not you? You're the only person who understands your morality threshold. How ambitious can you become? How ruthless can you be to those around you and still manage to sleep well at night as you work at making your dreams a reality? There's one job, one bonus, or one transfer, and five candidates are going for it. Four of the people applying for it are automatically doomed for disappointment. Do you have to be one of them? No, you don't.

The worst thing I've ever repeatedly done on the job was simply to stand out of the way and watch someone fall flat on her ass while knowing I could have saved her. I've never stolen anyone's ideas, belittled anyone, or cheated to get ahead. Some people think that, in business, it's occasionally necessary for you to throw someone under a bus to get ahead. It's not that I've never wanted to do this; it's just that I've never found the perfect moment to do it without getting caught. Fortunately for me, people in offices tend to shoot themselves in the foot or the head every day. Truth be told, I've done this to myself on numerous occasions. And if some of you out there are honest with yourselves, you know you've sabotaged one or two of your own opportunities as well. You've heard the expression, "Give 'em enough rope, and they'll hang themselves." Well, it's true. Give people in the office enough space and a running start, and they'll fly right off a cliff all on their own. The only thing you have to do in this situation is get out of their way. There were plenty of times, while watching someone make a costly mistake, that I turned my back and feigned cluelessness, knowing the whole time that her outcome would be most unpleasant. Yes, this is the height of passive-aggressive behavior, but I've seen others do much worse. Some people in the office will try to help you realize your dreams, but they're outnumbered by the people who see you as a threat to their own goals. If you want to reach the highest summit in business, my advice to you is to go on the offensive, and stay on the offensive. If you can live with the choices you made to get ahead, and you haven't done anything that would damage your future credibility, that's all that matters. If you can't, perhaps you should consider using some of your free time to do charity work to even out your karma.

Chapter 14

There Is More Than One Way Up

Have you ever watched a rugby game? If not, you really should. The first few times I watched the sport, I couldn't figure out how either team was able to score. It was illegal to throw a forward pass, and the ball was moved up the field through a series of lateral and backward passes that defied logic. It was like watching a clumsy, violent, and psychotic ballet performed the wrong way on a moving conveyor belt.

After watching a few games, I figured out how it worked. And after hitting a couple of obstacles as I progressed up the corporate ladder, I learned how a lack of forward momentum could actually help my career goals. Most corporations have something called a lateral promotion. There are two types. The first is an apples-to-apples promotion. Your new workload and responsibilities are comparable to those of your old position. This can be viewed as a *"title only"* promotion because the new job you'll be asked to do won't significantly change from your old job. The biggest change is what people call you in the office. For instance, a CSR (customer service representative), a UA (underwriting assistant), and a UTA (underwriting technical assistance) are all very similar, lateral jobs.

The second type is more like apples-to-coconuts. The new workload is extreme, and your responsibilities are greater than those of your previous job. You should get a raise, but because it's called a *lateral move*, you won't get any extra pay. These promotions are the most challenging to deal with. It's hard to focus on learning the new skills you need to perform the job while you're wondering how it could possibly be considered equivalent to your former function.

Both types of lateral moves can work to your advantage, if you know how to use them correctly. A lateral move can be a fresh start. It can take you out of a dead-end position and kick-start your career on a whole new path. You may need training to acquire a whole new skill set. And as we learned earlier, every experience counts on your résumé. If you were in a rut, a lateral move can get you out of it. It can open up new promotion opportunities, especially if you go along with the change willingly. A lateral move is a chance for you to show your supervisor or manager the stuff you're made of. And if you're having unresolved personal problems with a coworker, you can leave her and the problems in your old department. That is, unless the problems are mostly your own fault. In that case, you'll just end up taking your negative baggage with you wherever you go. But, if you find yourself being one half of a no-fault personality problem where you and a coworker can't get along and clash like fire and gasoline, a lateral move can be the quickest and safest way to diffuse the situation before it adversely affects your career.

You'll need to be both ambitious and flexible to make either of these lateral moves work. If it's an apples-to-coconuts move, you'll need to forgive your employer for choosing this path for you, and make the most of it. Be cautious, however; a lateral move that's forced upon you suddenly may be a subtle warning of things to come. If an employer can justify a lateral move once, they usually do it again and again, changing your job description and duties while robbing you of not only cash but opportunities. A lateral promotion without a pay increase is still considered a form of advancement. Some companies have a rule that an employee needs to be in a position six to twelve months before they can apply for another position. There's no telling how many opportunities for real career and financial growth you'll miss during that year.

Lateral promotions are sometimes experimental and can disappear as easily as they appear. I saw this happen once, and the unfortunate individual who was transferred from a defunct department into the disappearing job had nowhere to go but out the door. She was offered another position, but it came with a major pay decrease and offered no potential for career growth. We're talking a pay decrease well below the cost of living for herself, her unemployed husband, and their two children. The salary offered was barely above what she would have collected on unemployment, and if she had accepted it, her family would have faced a slow and very painful bleed toward financial ruin. Turning the offer down eliminated her chances of collecting unemployment, but it also stimulated her drive to find suitable employment elsewhere. She was able to find a good-paying job—a better job—well before her severance pay ran out. In the end, she benefited greatly by parting company with her ex-employer.

In even rarer cases, if you find yourself in a dead-end position, you can justify the creation of a lateral promotion—as long as you can show how it would benefit the company you work for. In this case, it would be best to sit down and write a proposal that shows the benefit of creating multiple lateral promotions. If you create only one, there's no guarantee that your supervisor or manager will automatically decide to fill it with you. When I worked as a mail clerk, I wanted a raise. My manager told me to write up a proposal. I think he thought I couldn't write one and would just back down. A week later I set up an appointment with him and explained why I thought I was due for a raise. And then I told him that, after thinking about it, I'd changed my mind. We were all due for raises. I pulled out a proposal and showed him where three new titles and promotions were needed and what he could expect each person to do in their new positions. He took the proposal and thought about it for a few weeks, then promoted everyone in the department. I created three positions for three people. I was assured of getting one of them.

For the record, I didn't really care if my coworkers got raises or not, nor did I believe they deserved them. I was just looking out for my own best interest.

If I'd created a promotion for myself, I might have accidentally become a working supervisor, and the men I worked with would have been upset about reporting to me, a woman. Mail rooms and supply departments have historically been the most male dominated areas within the corporate structure. When I was first promoted to the mail room, the guys went out of their way to let me know that I wasn't welcome there. One of our tasks was to move furniture. The clunky old desks this office used were huge monsters and required that at least two people work together to move them safely. When the guys were scheduled to move furniture, three of them at a time would show up and help each other out. When it was my turn to move furniture, the guys would all go to lunch together, or call in sick. I didn't think I could move the desks by myself, so I would wait until the guys came back to ask one of them for help, but they never would come back on the day I needed assistance. And the next day, everyone was too busy to help me, and my boss, who wasn't thrilled that a woman was in his department either, would threaten to write me up for failing to comply with my job functions. He told me that any one of the guys could move a desk by himself and that if I wanted to stay in the department I needed to step up my efforts. Of course he was right. I went home and thought about the problem. If the guys could move a desk by themselves, surely I could figure out a way to do it by myself as well.

One night while at home, I started to think about the process of moving one of these desks and I realized that I was repeatedly making two mistakes that prevented me for completing my task. First, I assumed I couldn't move the desk on my own. And second, I kept expecting guys who weren't happy about me being around to help me out. I had to rework this moving process and figure out how I could do the work by myself.

The desks were moved through the office on flat four-wheel carts. But this required that at least two people work together and lift the desk onto the cart. I knew I couldn't do that by myself, so I had to try using a two-wheel hand truck instead. The desks were L-shaped. The short end had to go on the bottom of the hand truck. The long end had to be braced against the frame. The hardest part was flipping the desk into position. But once I figured out how to brace the hand truck in place, it became easier.

The only flaw in my plan was that I was in such a hurry to get this job done that I didn't think about actually tying the desk to the cart. I had to move the desk slowly through the office so it wouldn't fall off the cart. It was a very delicate operation. This actually proved to be a good thing, because, although my arms got tired from supporting the weight of the desk, I didn't gouge any walls as I moved through the office. I did however cause a stir. My mail room coworkers were off somewhere laughing about the fact that I was going to get fired for not doing my job. But some of the other men in the office—oh, underwriters, claims adjusters, programmers—saw a woman moving an extremely heavy piece of furniture by herself, and they just lost it. A couple of guys in business suits started yelling at me to put the desk down. But I kept going because it was my job. They started yelling across the office to other men, telling them to make me stop. I was rushed by a small army of young men who wanted to know where the mail room guys were. And I told them that I was now one of the mail room guys, and I was just trying to do my job. And I did my best to keep moving. But when I rolled the desk past the vice president's office and he looked up and saw what I was doing the move stopped. He took the desk from me and had some of the other men in the office get a four-wheel cart. They hustled the desk onto it and moved it the last five hundred feet for me.

The mail room guys I worked with developed a whole new respect for me after that, but still not one of them would have wanted to call me boss. The only way I could get a promotion in the mail room was to make sure each of the guys got one as well. That way, I got what I wanted, and my coworkers got something too. They were happy with me for the remainder of my stay in that department, which lasted only two weeks, because I immediately got promoted to a different department. But that's another story for another book.

Chapter 15

Find the Weakest Gazelle, but Think before You Eat It

Remember when I said that the highest form of passive-aggressive behavior was purposely letting a coworker trip over his own feet and fall off a cliff? Well, it's not. There's something far worse and totally shameful, but if you believe that all's fair in love, war, and business this strategy may be of benefit to you somewhere down the line.

Business is not just about survival of the fittest; it's also about survival of the smartest. The fittest are those people bred to work in business, people sent by their parents to the best schools, people coming from wealthy families, people who are, in other words, to the manor born. The smartest are those people who come up with the most innovative way to get around their own shortcomings and who stop letting their circumstances get in the way of their success. The smartest people are fighters. To successfully ascend the corporate ladder, you've got to be a predator, a wolf in sheep's clothing. You need to identify the weakest people next to you or above you and pick them off the ladder one body at a time, clearing a path for yourself as you go along. Few people are born at the top of the ladder, and not everyone born at the bottom stays there. What happens to the people in between is never pretty, but battles in the animal kingdom seldom are.

While you're looking for your next promotion or bonus, you occasionally will run into what I call the "weak gazelles," the people most likely to be eaten by a bear in the wild. That's cruel. What I actually mean is that these people are a bit too Bohemian for business. They appear timid and clueless and are probably content to stay exactly where they are within the corporation. Their only problem may be that they're directly in your path. By societal standards, these people are classified as underachievers. By societal standards, anyone who's content with the status quo of anything is an underachiever. These employees may be close to retirement and just looking for a place to lay low until that day arrives. If they've been at the company forever, coming to work may be more of a social event to them now than a means of income. They may already have two pensions under their belts. It's not unusual to find people who have retired from the post office or other government jobs spending their golden years working in a corporate mail room. Sometimes these people have stayed in a position so long that they end up getting on their boss's last nerve. These people have a habit of clogging the pipes; fresh blood can't circulate into a department if long-term workers refuse to leave.

Your first instinct may be to try to pick these people off. It's easy to do. Usually a few conversations about grandchildren growing up fast, or travel, or relaxation can get them into a retirement frame of mind. If they're too young to retire, maybe they've never considered what the extra income from a new promotion can do financially for their lives. They may need someone like you to do the math for them.

Before you do knock them off the ladder, though, it may be of better advantage to you to do something that no one would expect: drag them up the food chain with you. Am I suggesting you use them as a human shield? Heavens, no (she says, as she shakes her head yes)! Well, not exactly. First you should simply use them as a cover. No matter how stealthy you are on your way to the top, someone is bound to notice what you're doing after a while. The people at the top plan to stay there and are keeping an eye out for young challengers such as you. But they're not looking out for tag teams. Drag that weak gazelle kicking and screaming up the corporate ladder with you. For a time, she will reap the benefits of such an association—bonuses, promotions, great work reviews, and so on. And it's easy to help them out. A bit of prodding is usually all that's required to get them to take the first step of going on an intra-office job interview. Unless they're totally inept, they usually can get almost any job they go for because they've been so ambitiously inactive on the job that it shocks everyone when they finally decide to try something new. A supervisor will usually rush to place a weak gazelle in a new position before she has a chance to think about it and change her mind about taking the job. Once she gets that promotion, she'll look to you for future guidance. She's now yours to mold into any form you choose.

It may sound like I'm crazy for encouraging you to assist someone else with their career, but climbing the corporate ladder is a lot of hard work, no matter how you do it. Sometimes it's more to your advantage to invest a little of your effort into the people around you, instead of just focusing on yourself. You never know when having a ready-made ally can come in handy.

The weak gazelle didn't initially ask for your help and may now be in over her head. Because you insisted she take this career move, it's up to you to do whatever it takes to keep her from drowning. Like it or not, she is linked to you. Her successes and failures are also yours. If you can protect the weak gazelle on her way up the corporate ladder, people will look at you not with suspicion but with awe. They won't see an ambitious person selfishly trying to climb the corporate ladder for personal gain. No, they'll see you as a mentor, as a person sure enough of herself in her own job that she can take time to help out a colleague. You're using the weak gazelle as a diversion. People will be more interested in how your mentee performs in her new role and won't pay attention to what you're doing behind the scenes.

Again, this sounds like a lot of work, and it is. After all, you could just worry about getting up the corporate ladder yourself and reduce the amount of effort it's going to take to get you there by not dragging along a sidekick. However, keep in mind that you're looking for opportunities for advancement anywhere and everywhere, even creating your own opportunities if you have to as you go along. The weak gazelle is not only your mentee. She's also your trainee. And you've successfully (and with very little effort I might add) concocted a scenario in which you are not merely helping another employee, you're managing another employee. You're giving the people around you a little taste of your supervisory skills. You've created a situation that lets you flaunt and even improve your leadership abilities. Remember, in an office, people are always watching you. You never know which supervisors or managers are looking for new talent for their departments. Why not give them a show?

If you've planned it right, the two of you will wind up within the same department. And the position she gets should be equal to yours or lower. If you can learn to do the job correctly, there's no reason why you can't have lunch with her every day and give her some hints to make the job easy for her.

Eventually, the new job will become as routine to her as her former job was, and she'll happily settle into her new function. If it came with a salary increase, she'll forgive you from dislodging her from her former pattern. There have been several occasions on which I've been surprised by weak gazelles who just needed a bit of prodding to move along. In these cases, the employees stumbled a little but got up on their feet, and then, once they realized the advantages of actually changing departments, they became my greatest competition and gave me a run for my money.

What you've done here is created a cohort, the importance of which we'll discuss in a later chapter. But this particular cohort will be the best you'll ever have. She's successful now. She has more earning power.

And she'll retire at a higher pay grade... all thanks to you. If you need help with any future schemes, this will be your go-to person. She will be your extra set of eyes and ears. And in the corporate jungle, it's important to have friends, even artificial ones.

When you've helped your coworker up the ladder as far as you can or you need to focus more on your own career path or you need another diversion, cut the weak gazelle loose. Let your paths naturally diverge. If the association between the two of you has lasted for a few years, she will, more than likely, land on her feet. And should she want to climb the corporate ladder on her own, hopeful her association with you will have taught her a trick or two.

Chapter 16
Unwitting Corporate Tool

I've prodded several weak gazelles into moving into different department, but I've only dislodged one out of a position she desperately want to keep, and it wasn't anything I intended to do. When I was in the records department I was young and foolish. I developed a taste for cash but not for work. I was impulsive and into instant gratification. Advancement was a rush, and adrenaline has always been my drug of choice. The company I worked for unwittingly fed my cash addiction by giving me bonuses for every little thing I did. If I didn't get the raises and perks I wanted, I lashed out like a spoiled brat. But I also schemed. I came up with innovative ways to get the things I wanted. I pitted people against each other in the hopes someone would quit and free up more cash for me. I badgered my boss for raises. I badgered my clients for good reviews. My supervisor figured out that I was capable of just about anything when it came to getting what I wanted. What she wondered was whether or not I was capable of just about anything to get what she wanted.

I was looking to get out of the records department. I could have gone to the rating department, but I looked at how much work was involved for that type of position and realized I wasn't mature enough yet to accept the responsibilities. So instead, I opted for a lateral promotion to the mail room. All I needed was my supervisor's approval to be able to apply for a current open position there. Since she really didn't like me very much, I assumed that getting her approval would be the easiest thing to do. So I went and asked her.

My supervisor took me into a room, and I thought we were going to discuss me wanting to leave the department, but she didn't say anything. I didn't know where to start the conversation, so I just waited for her to say something. But she didn't. I cleared my throat. Nothing. I finally said that I wanted to apply for a position in the mail room. She replied that she wanted a particular woman out of the records department— we'll call her Kelly.

"Kelly" was a really sweet, naive woman who was a lot like the character Betty White played in *Golden Girls*. In fact I think she might even have been from Minnesota too. She had worked in the records department for twenty years, and her supervisor wanted her out. Kelly operated at one pace—slow. She never came up with any ideas about how to improve work flow, she was the slowest at learning new procedures, and she almost had a breakdown when the department got a computer (an old CRT that predated desktops, laptops, and iPads) and started to automate itself. Change frightened Kelly. It spooked her like thunder spooks sheep. She was content to stay in the records department for as long as she lived. But our supervisor had had enough of her, and it was time for her to go. One way or another.

Our supervisor told me that if I wanted the promotion to the mail room (which I did) I had to get Kelly out of the department first. Otherwise, she would never give her consent for me to transfer anywhere. I could spend my days in the record department, and Kelly and I could have a contest to see who retired from there first. I was only twenty-four years old, and although I was reasonably sure Kelly would retire first, I didn't want to stick around and find out. My supervisor told me she knew exactly what I was capable of and if anyone could get Kelly out of the department, it was me.

I went home angry. I didn't want to stay in the department, but I didn't want to push Kelly into taking a job she didn't want. I knew she was content in the records department. But I wasn't. I had a weekend to think about it, and I decided that Kelly needed a new job. First I asked her about her current job and how she liked it. She told me she loved everything about it except our boss. She confided in me that she was just trying to wait her out. She hoped our boss, who was much older than her, would decide to retire. Maybe her replacement would be more humane. This was all I needed to know.

I started working on Kelly, trying to make her doubt that staying in the department was a good idea. It was hard to work on her without making her paranoid. The only job available at that moment was in the rating department. Our boss had put in a good word for her. All she had to do was apply, and the job was hers. But she didn't think she could do the job and was afraid if she took it she'd get fired. Under normal circumstances, she would have been right, but I wasn't about to let that happen. I felt sorry for her, but I knew if she didn't take that job, not only would I not get a promotion, but it was only a matter of time before our boss would figure out a legitimate way to fire her.

I worked on her every day, telling her how great a job in the rating department would be and how nice her new coworkers would be. And when none of this worked, I finally introduced her to the writing on the wall and I told her bluntly it was this job or eventual unemployment. And I promised to have her back. Kelly applied for the job and got it and was immediately overwhelmed. I got the new job in the mail room, but I couldn't leave Kelly to drown. I didn't have the heart.

So I approached her supervisor and said that even though I had just received a promotion to the mail room, I eventually wanted to move to the rating department and I asked if there were any courses I could take or training I could receive that would make me a better candidate for the job. I was able to take self-study courses on insurance operations, rating functions, and insurance rating. I read through the courses quickly but only found them to be minimally helpful. I asked other people who were already in the department to keep an eye on Kelly until I could get to the department and help her myself. People thought I was crazy, but a year later, there I was a commercial lines rater. Kelly was still in the department struggling. I came up behind her and helped her as much as I could. I learned every shortcut I could and taught her how to improve her production numbers by hook or by crook. Kelly was still understandably angry with me for initially trying to trick her into taking the promotion in the first place. It was hard to get her to trust me again, but she was getting heat from her supervisor for being slow, so she needed help, even my help.

I got other people in the department to agree to help her become more productive. She was not the most compliant student you could want to teach, but eventually she got it. And when the job became easier for her to do, she was happy that she had it. She actually started to get decent pay increases for the first time in a long time.

I remained in that department for two years. My next move was a job at another company. I made sure that Kelly had mentors to look out for her. I stayed at the company long enough to see our evil records boss retire. Both Kelly and I had outlasted her at the corporation, and in the end that was all that mattered—that, and the oath I took to let weak gazelles lie.

Chapter 17

A Different Weak Gazelle

Sometimes weak gazelle are weak not because of their own flaws, but due to the narrow vision of the people around them. These unfortunate people usually find themselves in jobs they're more than capable of performing, but they're unlucky enough to have been put with the wrong group, people incapable of working together. After being a rater for three years, I changed companies and wound up working back in the Chicago Loop at a company housed in the Willis Tower (the building formerly known as the Sears Tower). I worked there for a few years and was quite happy, until we got a new supervisor. She had been recruited into the company through a job fair and was fresh out of college. She was very, very young. I'm not sure if she'd ever had a job before, let alone any supervisory experience. I wasn't that much older than her and had never wanted to be a supervisor, but I found myself immediately jealous of this woman. It was hard for me to take instructions from someone ten or more years my junior.

I wasn't alone. The other eight people in the department felt exactly the same way. The only difference between me and the other employees in the department was how we decided to handle the situation. Me, I did my job, was as polite to our new boss as I could be, listened to everything she said, followed her instructions, but I did everything I possibly could to avoid her. I limited our interaction. I didn't want her as a boss or as a friend. The other raters talked about her behind her back, argued with her about everything she said, and refused to give her new ideas a chance.

Betty (as we'll call her) was a very upbeat person and somehow managed to keep her composure no matter what her subordinates said to her. However, two weeks after she started the job, I found her in one of the bathroom stalls crying her eyes out. Between sobs she told me that the other people in the department hated her. She was starting to second guess her decision to accept this job. And she wondered why the other raters couldn't be more like me and give her at least half a chance to prove herself. She looked like she needed a hug and someone to tell her that everything would turn out OK in the end. I realized at that moment that my boss was the equivalent of a corporate toddler. She started this job without first knowing how to walk and didn't have a support group to help her transition smoothly into her role as a manager. She had no clue what to do with the people in her unit, including me. I couldn't believe she was that helpless. Upper management had thrown her into the deep end of a shark-infested pool and told her to basically sink or swim. And either way, she was chum.

I'm ambitious, but I'm not completely heartless. I didn't expect to find my boss crying alone in the bathroom. It was then that I realized how awful I had been. I was jealous of her not because of her job or her salary. I was jealous of her because she was young. It wasn't her fault I was born a decade before she was. I felt that I had to help her, and I told her I would some-way, but I wasn't at all sure how. I talked to the other raters in the unit, but I couldn't get one of them to cut the new kid any slack. I tried to reason with them, but after two weeks of running the new supervisor into the ground, they were having too much fun to quit stomping on her.

Betty was pushed into the role of being a weak ga-zelle by the very workers she was supposed to con-trol. I was ashamed that I allowed petty jealousy to cloud my opinion of this young yet highly intelligent colleague and felt that I needed to make amends for being indifferent to her as a human being. I told her to brace herself at the next department meeting because it was going to be caustic, and no matter what hap-pened, she shouldn't act surprised.

A week later we had a department meeting. Betty introduced some changes to the work flow that she wanted to implement immediately. There was a lot of grumbling, and one of the more vocal raters simply stated she wasn't going to change the way she did her job. The others agreed with her and also refused to make any changes. They started hurling insults at Betty (mostly about her age and inexperience). Betty did her best not to react, but I could see her composure crack-ing. I took a slow, deep breath, and then bellowed,

"Hey, shut up already." And then I screeched, "You're giving me a headache."

I'm normally as Zen as a non-Buddhist can be. But I had to get their attention, and being rude was the best way to do it. All eyes turned my way. I didn't really have a plan and had to ad-lib the rest of my tirade.

"Great," I said. "I get that you aren't impressed with our new boss and that you really don't want to do any extra work. Who does?"

One of my colleagues opened her mouth to say something.

"No, don't you talk right now," I said. "Don't even think about talking. You people really are giving me a headache, and I'm tired of you. If you don't want to listen to Betty, then don't. You're grown adults being paid to work for this woman. If you don't want to do that, why don't you quit now?"

A couple of them shifted in their seats. And one brave soul got ready to make a comment.

I just held up my hand. "No, really, don't say anything. That was a rhetorical question. I don't really care about what's going on in your head. Just listen. I want to keep my job. Betty is going to explain the new procedures to me. I'm going to do the work. If it frees up my time like she says it will, I'll do someone else's work too. I don't know about any of you, but I'm keeping my job. And you people can go pound sand."

Then I turned to Betty and asked if I could be excused to get some aspirin. By then I did have a headache. For the next three months, our department meetings went like that. Someone would make a crack about not wanting to listen to Betty, and I would just go off like I was a rabid dog. But Betty's ideas were really good. I was able to do my work in record time and help out other people. When my coworkers saw how easy the job was becoming, they tried the new procedures too and loved them. All but one rater developed a new respect for our boss. That one rater found a job at another company. She told me she was just too old to change, and after fifteen years on the job, she just didn't feel like taking directions from a child.

Betty's ideas were now readily adopted. But the best part about the whole thing for me was that I was able to help her behind the scenes. She would run her ideas by me and I would create experiments to test the procedures and make sure they generated the desired outcome. Many procedures had to be redeveloped multiple times before they actually worked. Then, and only then, they would be released to the entire rating department for use. The other raters had no idea how much work went into streamlining our new work flow.

Betty was our supervisor for two years and then was transferred to one of the company's suburban offices. She asked me to go with her. She was sure she wouldn't have any friends out there and needed some support. I told her that we were the roughest crowd the company had and if she could survive us, the employees at the new office would be a snap to handle. Then I called a few friends in that office and asked them to keep an eye on her. Betty missed me for a while, but it was just as I had told her. The people in her new department were a lot more civil than we had been.

Chapter 18

Sometimes It's Like Playing Marbles

Very few promotions happen at corporations where an employee moves into a brand-new, previously nonexistent position. Most of the time the spot once was held by someone else and was vacated one way or another. People get promoted, quit, are fired or downsized, and even die. In rare cases, though, they're knocked out of their spots by other, viciously ambitious employees and they just never even see it coming.

As you shift jobs around the office, you occasionally will find one you want or need for advancement that's already filled with a warm body. There are very few ways you can actively get someone out of a spot without making yourself appear cruel and monstrous. One person's ambition is another person's selfishness. How easy do you think it is to take another person's position away, and what do you think your coworkers will think of you once you do?

While in the office, all you can do is try your best to look like a better candidate for that job. While this tactic sometimes works, it requires the patience of a saint, as you may literally wait years to be considered for a filled position. And even then, it only works if the employee you're trying to replace starts having problems on the job and is suddenly in danger of being sacked. Outside the company, however, there is a lot you can do.

🏮 Work on Them after Hours

Even the most subtle people have problems doing things under office scrutiny. To convince someone to vacate a job, sometimes it's best to work on them after hours, over drinks, or at a social event like a party. To do this, you'll first have to know if the person is happy in her job, near retirement, has other options, or muses about pursuing a new career or an education. Once you know what makes a person tick, it's easy to figure out how to have a conversation with her that triggers her desire to move on. If she doesn't want to leave her job, however, no amount of prodding from you over cocktails is going to make a difference. You'll have to find another way.

🏮 Become the Drama

If you don't mind hurting someone, you can always quietly stir up some office drama. When a person leaves on her own accord without a new job lined up, it's usually because something in the office environment is pushing her to want out. I'm not a fan of this method, but it is effective. Just play on her insecurities and make her a little paranoid. Or if she's having personal problems with another employee, try pushing that person's buttons to see what happens.

It's easy to fuel an office feud, but it's hard to do it without getting hit by the fallout. If you're good at instigating drama, let it rip. I've seen huge blowouts happen in an office, and when the melee was over, no one could figure out how it all began, although you can sometimes catch a glimpse of someone smirking in the background when the dust settles. This tactic has a tendency to create bad feelings that linger around the office for a long time, because not everyone involved in the drama leaves. If you think you can work it to your advantage, use it, but be careful. Most people who read this will consider this approach to be immoral and repulsive, and I agree; I'm not a fan of this approach. But it does happen in offices more than you think. If you can avoid engaging in this sort of behavior, please do. Corporations are great examples of how small the world really is. As you move from company to company, some of the same people you work with today will move with you, will move after you, or will precede you. And they all have extremely long memories. Be careful not to burn too many bridges in your quest for advancement.

🗞 Job Hunt on Their Behalf

Nothing motivates a person to change jobs faster than a better offer somewhere else. The problem is that very few people will look for a job somewhere else when they're comfortable in the positions they have. Although a pay increase and better benefits are always nice, the hassle of retraining and reestablishing oneself at a new job sometimes makes the career move seem very unattractive. It takes just the right perks to entice an entrenched employee out of her job. As a last resort, if a coworker has a job you want but is reluctant to leave it, you can job hunt on her behalf and find her another job even better than the one she currently has. The hardest part with this option is to figure out exactly what it would take to budge her from her current job. I've done this twice and was amazed when it worked. The first time I did it, I job hunted for an underwriting assistant that I just didn't want around the company anymore.

Christina (not her real name) had figured out my modus operandi and was blocking my chance of promotion to her department even though I wasn't directly after her job. She didn't appreciate my form of ambition. I wasn't motivated by the pride of doing a good job or the sense of accomplishment you get by being recognized as a hard worker by your peers. No, I was interested only in lots of cold, hard cash. I went after every promotion, drop of overtime, and bonus that I could find. I had reached my growth potential in the mail room and needed to break in to another department. The logical step was commercial lines rating. My nemesis had to go.

Now, what I'm about to tell you is something that a very young, foolish, spoiled brat did in order to get a job she wanted. It blows right through all the gray areas of ethics and into the zones of criminality. And I only mention it here because it had a happy ending for all parties concerned. It's not anything I suggest you do, because it's nothing short of one of the most bizarre cases of identity theft in US history that you'll ever hear about. Please, under no circumstances do this at home.

My company had a policy that discouraged employees from talking to headhunters while on company time—it was grounds for immediate termination. It occurred to me that the quickest way to get Christina out of the picture was to get her to talk to a headhunter while in the office. I called around and found a supervisory position available at an insurance company in a suburb not far from where she lived. I knew that although she loved her current job, she hated every minute of her daily commute to the Chicago Loop, the cost of parking, and the crowded commuter trains she had to take whenever driving just wasn't an option. I didn't have the skills required for the job; otherwise I might have gone for it myself. All I had to do was pretend I was her, call and leave a message, and give them her work number. I called after I got home at around nine in the evening to ensure that I wouldn't have to talk to a live person. I knew I couldn't pull it off if I actually talked to a live person and for my scheme to work I needed them to call her back. I said I wanted more information about the job before I considered applying for it. I think I even said I wanted to discuss the salary, because I thought it was a bit low. I explained my skills (her skills), my educational background (her educational background), and told them they should call me if they were serious about finding the right candidate for the job. I thought if I was cocky enough, they would at least call back just to tell me how much of a bitch I was being.

I wasn't thinking about what it would mean to Christina to lose her job because of a lie or what it would mean to my company for wrongly firing an employee. Christina had taunted me for a year and prevented me repeatedly from obtaining a promotion I wanted. She didn't realize how immature I was, how flawed my logic could be, or what I was capable of.

The next morning Christina got several calls about a job she never applied for. I was near her desk when one such call came in. She glanced around, afraid that someone would hear her as she desperately told the person on the other end that she had never called him about a job and had no idea what he was talking about. People around her were starting to glance in her direction. This was going to be good. At some point, the caller must have skipped to what the position paid, because instantly her fear changed into intrigue. She asked for their number and then excused herself from the office. Under the company's guidelines, that was acceptable. She applied for the job, discreetly went on an interview, then a second one, and shocked everyone (but me) when she put in her two weeks' notice. I think she knew I had something to do with it, because she started giving me strange looks, like she wondered just how far I was willing to go to get my own way. I wish I had an answer for her, but I didn't. And I still don't. I've never reached that limit.

Although what I did was definitely the wrong thing for the wrong reason, job hunting for another person is still a great way to get someone who's purposely being an obstacle out of your way. In today's job market, you no longer have to pretend to be them. Head hunters are hungry for new leads. You can legally throw them a bone by giving them a coworker's name and phone number. Make sure the job comes with a salary and perks that will entice her to apply for the job. And just keep your fingers crossed that she gets it.

I did this a second time to "help" a supervisor find a lucrative position far, far away from me. I didn't pretend to be her. But I did pretend to have the skills required to do the job. I called a recruiter and discussed an available position with him. After we talked about the salary and benefits, I decide that the job just wasn't for me. The recruiter asked if I had any friends I thought would be interested in the job, and it just so happened that I did. I recommended my supervisor. The difference this time was that I went into the office and told my supervisor that I didn't know if she was currently looking for a new job, but I'd heard about a position she'd be perfect for. I hoped she wasn't angry with me, but I did recommend her for the job and I gave the recruiter her work number. She should be getting a call about a great job soon. She, like Christina, ended up going on an interview and taking a lucrative position elsewhere. And my next supervisor was everything I could wish for—supportive, kind, and savvy. I spent the remainder of my stay at that company as a very happy camper.

📓 Use Your Cohorts and Mentors

No one in corporate America is self-made. Whether someone actively assists you, or you take it upon yourself to use others around you as stepping-stones to bigger and better things, you won't make it up the corporate ladder on your own. Someone will train you, someone else will inspire you, yet another person will be an example of how you shouldn't behave if you want to succeed, and someone else will be the role model of your dreams. You'll find support in some of the most unlikely places. And whenever you find someone willing to help you along your corporate journey, hang on to her for dear life.

American Country Insurance Company had its own specific way of processing work. This company was one of the most paper-orientated companies I'd ever worked for. I thought I was doing a good job filling out the paperwork, but a data-entry clerk and coder named Cenora came up to me one day and pointed out some serious mistakes I was making—mistakes that other coders were content to ignore and that could cost me my job. I was grateful to her for bringing them to my attention. I would take Cenora out to lunch occasionally and do whatever I could to keep her happy. It was rare to find someone at this company, or any company, that was willing to help out a colleague. We've been friends now for fifteen years.

Before I discovered the value of having cohorts, I resorted to bribery to keep the people around me in line, and I frequently offered my colleagues cash to get them to do their jobs properly. This is the lazy person's method of personnel management. I was in a supervisory position that had absolutely no power behind the title. I was new to the department, and my coworkers didn't realize that any changes I came up with were solely to make the job easier. I'm not talking about cutting corners. I could look at any step in our work flow, treat it like a logic problem, and if there was a faster, more efficient, and easier way to accomplish it, I would find it. But because my methods involved change, everyone in my department also assumed it meant more work, and they would balk at every suggestion I made.

That's when I resorted to bribery. I would usually challenge the department to try the new procedure, and anyone who didn't like it could get twenty dollars for at least being a sport. It worked. All the clerks tried my new procedures, desperately trying to find flaws with my changes. But most people found the changes to be as good as I said they'd be. A couple of people refused to like the changes and demanded the twenty dollars. I'm not one to renege on a promise, and since it was only two people, I paid them. About a week later, the cash was returned. It seems that although they took the money, they really liked my ideas and not only used them, but started pushing me to come up with more ideas. I kept offering bribes until my co-workers got so used to my ideas that they told me enticements weren't necessary. They knew if I told them something was easy, it was.

Working at American Country Insurance Company (ACIC) drove home the importance of cohorts. Cenora and I had started working at the company around the same day. There were several of us who went through orientation together. We were all newbies in our departments. We were all teased by our new coworkers and only felt at peace when we were in the company of our own small group. We bonded together, because no other established group would have us in the first few months we worked there. Even after our newness wore off, we were never as close to other coworkers as we were to each other.

Another group of cohorts developed when Cenora and I both discovered that there was a group of people in our department who were all born in the same year. We all grew up listening to pretty much the same music, reading the same books, watching the same TV programs, but more importantly, we shared milestone birthdays. In a few years, we all would be turning fifty. We had more in common than most people in the office, and we looked out more for each other too. We also fought at times as if we were real siblings, but that happens to the closest of people. We supported each other, trained each other, and protected each other because we were close. We also had fun together, something that's rare in an office.

If I wasn't hanging out with one of my cohorts, I could be found with the person at the company I had picked as a mentor. Most of the corporations I worked for had mandatory mentoring programs in which they would assign a mentor to show a new employee the ropes. I preferred to make my own choice of mentor because I'd be spending a vast amount of time with that person.

Mentors are supposed to acclimate their mentees to the company rules, regulations, and philosophies, but they also can help you choose a career path and show you how to start succeeding in your chosen field. They can tell you who you need to get to know and who you need to avoid. They can suggest classes for you to take and even help you improve your outward image. My first few mentors had a rough time with me because I was all about instant gratification. I would see a job or bonus I wanted, try a few things to get it, fail, and then throw a tantrum because I didn't get my way. When I was younger, I had a problem of always expecting things to be easier than they actually were. I found it frustrating to have to make an effort to accomplish a task. My mentors tried to explain to me the virtues of patience, but they were talking to a twenty-something-year-old. You can't party with patience, right? You can't drink with it, can't eat with it—not like you can with cash. I was young, foolish, selfish, and anything but patient. Over the years, my mentors were able to help me alter my need for instant gratification, but I don't think they'd appreciate what that need has become today. The opposite of instant gratification is delayed gratification. I've developed the ability to wait for the right opportunity to get the things I want. I'm actually greedier now than I've ever been. I want wealth *and* power. And instead of throwing a tantrum or becoming angry about not getting immediate satisfaction, I've turned into a stalker. I can now bide my time until something I want becomes available, no matter how long it takes, and then pounce on it before anyone else has a chance at it.

Chapter 19

Your First Bid at an Internal Promotion

After working at a corporation for a while, you should start looking in every department for promotion opportunities. Ideally, when you finally find one, you'll be the only one aware of this opportunity. While working in an office with more than three hundred employees, I once saw an entire department go after the same job. The fighting that ensued was unlike anything I'd ever seen before. The position was shut down eventually in order to keep the peace, but the devastation caused by the department-wide competition permanently broke the team dynamic that had once existed, and many friendships were ruined.

More than likely, whenever you go up for a promotion within your office, there will be a minimum of four other people going for the same job, unless you work in a very small office. Of those four, two people are merely going for it because they want more money. They may have been turned down for raises and see a promotion as the only way to get more cash, and they're usually right. It hasn't occurred to either of these people that extra work is involved in order to get that extra money. Should either of these workers get the job, they usually won't last long in the position. I've seen this happen repeatedly through the years. Typically within two weeks, the promoted employee begs for her old job back, and in most cases she'll be accommodated, unless a replacement has already been hired. On rare occasions, she'll get fired. Look for these people every time a position becomes available. They're great fun to watch and provide hours of free entertainment. Their behavior is quite unpredictable. They'll try anything to keep the new position except actually doing the work. Additionally, if you wait a week or two you'll be able to reapply for the position such people can't wait to vacate.

One person will be exactly what the position needs: a current employee who's been on the job for a long time and who probably already does the work without the title or compensation. By accepting the responsibilities without asking for further compensation, however, this hapless person unfortunately has painted herself into a corner. If she was meant to have that job, it would already be hers. She won't get the job, because her boss has decided she's too valuable in her current position to promote. Like it or not, this employee has been forced into a niche. You'd think that a grateful employer, knowing that there's a capable employee who's demonstrated that she can do the job, would give it to her, but no. It usually doesn't happen that way. Still, she can't legally be discouraged from applying for the job or any other job within the company. But her application is usually given little consideration. This person will usually be stuck in a dead-end job. She'll have to get used to the idea of working at her current company forever with no chance of advancement, or she'll have to seek employment at another firm. Immediate supervisors usually have to give their permission for an employee to apply for a job in another department. I've seen people break down and cry when the answer is no. If you find yourself in this position, no matter how long you've been on the job you have, leave.

After becoming a commercial lines rater, the next logical step for me should have been to become an underwriting assistant. But at the moment I was ready to make my career move, my company experienced a severe loss. The bulk of the underwriters in the commercial lines department quit en masse. Disgruntled doesn't even begin to describe this group. They were so unhappy with their workloads, salaries, bonuses, and educational benefits that they planned and executed a scheme to quit roughly on the same day. Eight people on the professional staff just up and disappeared. Faced with such an instant depletion of their underwriting staff, managers scrambled to strengthen their workforce. At first they tried to hire in underwriters wherever they could find them. But no one wanted to come to work for a company that had lost 90 percent of its top producers on the same day.

The company's only recourse was to promote its raters to underwriter trainees and push them through a crash underwriting program, which was much like forcing them to run a gauntlet. But not everyone was that lucky. I had the highest production figures in the department, and my supervisor begged me to pass up this training period and promised me there'd be another. They needed trainees, but they also needed someone to process the work. I was heartbroken about the company's decision to make me pass on the opportunity, but I had no other option than to wait for the second round of training. So me and another hapless rater became the rating department and watched our coworkers head off to new careers.

What happened next can only be described as six months of living hell. The two of us became punching bags for the entire office. Overtime was unlimited, but even if there had been forty-eight hours in each day, we wouldn't have been able to keep up with the work flow any better. We were outnumbered eight to one by underwriter trainees, claims adjusters, and accountants all desperate to get timely quotes, issues, and endorsements. The other woman threatened to quit, and I told her she'd never get out of the company alive if she tried. A week later I threatened to do the same thing, and she threatened to slap me if I didn't shut up.

We were both given offices to work from and were allowed to close the doors for privacy and serenity. When I chose to keep my door open, people came in and screamed at me, broke down and cried in front of me, and swore under their breath or at the top of their lungs. I'm amazed my hair didn't turn completely white. And the work kept rolling in.

The first training session ended, and I prepared to join the second round. But this time, the company hired college graduates recruited from local universities to go directly into the underwriting program. They hired five new commercial lines rater trainees and left me right where I was so I could train them.

I had never been so disappointed in my life. Yes, I had been well compensated for my time during the six-month mad rush to enter policies, but the driving force behind my hard work wasn't the money. It had been the promise of specialized training and a fast track to an underwriting career. I was asked to train the new personnel, and I tried, but my heart just wasn't in it. It took me thirty days to find a new job as an underwriting assistant at an insurance broker. I lost a week's worth of vacation time annually, but in exchange, I got a five-thousand-dollar annual increase, my own small book of business, an Illinois Property and Casualty Producers Licenses, an Illinois Brokers License, and a whole new set of career opportunities.

The last person you want applying for the same job as you is a wild card. She might be applying because she saw everyone else doing it, and she wants to throw her hat into the ring too. Maybe she's been in the department for a while and has finally gotten up the courage to go for it. Maybe she really wants the job and feels her shot at it is as good as anyone else's. Or maybe she's doing it just because she can. Whatever her rationale, this person can be a real threat to your bid to get this job. She may not be the best candidate for the job, but her newfound ambition and longevity on the job can make her a more attractive candidate than you. The good news is that the only thing standing between you and this job isn't your coworkers; it's the job interview that will make all the difference.

Every person applying within a company for a promotion goes through an interview process, and very few people understand that even though they already work for the company, they still have to compete for the new position. They think that their job skills and past service record speak for themselves. But you all are applying for a new job. Under these circumstances, the playing field is leveled for everybody. You all have to start the process from scratch. Past experience won't be relevant if the new job is vastly different from the old one. Look at an interview for a new position at your current company the same way you'd look at a job interview for a new company. Decide how badly you want it, and then make it happen.

Besides reminding you to relax and be cool about the interview, the one thing I can tell you is that you need to understand the job responsibilities and make sure you can handle them before you apply. If skills are required that you don't have, figure out a way you can get them without a cost being incurred by the company. Find someone reliable who has the skills you need, and broker a deal with her for off-the-clock training. Make the deal contingent on your getting the job, unless you really want to learn skills you may not immediately use. If you can acquire new skills before you get a job instead of waiting for company training, you'll be ahead of the game.

I was approached at one company by a typist who had applied six times for a job in my department and didn't get it. The last time she had applied, she was told she lacked the necessary skills to perform the job. That was true, but it also was unfair. Every other candidate that had applied for and won similar jobs lacked the necessary skills to do those jobs until they were properly trained. In essence she was told politely that they didn't want to waste time training her. She came to me for help.

I started training her during my lunch period. We were both off the clock but processing real work. My supervisor came by and wanted to know what we were doing. I didn't see the harm in telling her the truth, so I explained the training. I thought it was a good thing that a typist wanted to learn how to help out in the rating department and eventually transfer to the department on a permanent basis. The woman was smart, efficient, diligent, and good-natured. She was exactly the kind of person you would want to have working with you. When my supervisor told me that the typist wasn't authorized to work in the policy issuance system and had to stop training immediately, I was shocked. I asked how the typist could get authorization, and my supervisor told me she couldn't. I disagreed with her, and the dispute went to our manager. He agreed with my supervisor and also insisted that I immediately stop training the typist. I was once again reminded of the corporate chain of command, on which I was the lowest rung, and was issued a verbal warning to cease and desist the training.

It would have ended there had I bothered to listen to anyone. I didn't. I rarely do. Training became covert. It was performed at the crack of dawn before the managers, or anyone who trafficked in gossip, came to work. It was performed late at night. We would leave and come back to the office around six forty-five, when most of the staff had already taken off. We had accomplices who helped us. Someone else would let us in so we wouldn't have to swipe our door access cards. And we weren't alone. More typists found out what we were doing, and they also wanted training. Soon I was training three people and checking their work, assigning them homework, and correcting their errors.

I created manuals that could have been called *Rating Insurance Policies for Dummies*. Everyone got a copy. I asked them to take them home, study them, and then show me what they learned from them the following business day. When we could get access to a test system, we'd use it instead of the live production program. When we couldn't use the test program, we'd log in to the live program as another worker who needed a boost to her production figures and would process the work under her name.

When the next position came available, the typist who'd approached me first went for it. The others agreed to leave it alone to allow her a chance to get the job. Again she was turned down, but it wasn't for lack of skills. It was because the other person applying had more seniority at the company, and they wanted to accommodate her. I thought it was wrong, because I knew the typist now had the better skills, but she actually was happy about what happened. She told me that it felt good because they could no longer turn her down because of a skills deficit. She thanked me for the training and walked away. A month later she was the newest rater at a different company. And shortly after that, my other two trainees found rating positions elsewhere as well. I was flooded by requests to provide rater training to people in almost every entry-level position in the company. I managed to train a few more before I wasn't allowed to hang out with my coworkers anymore. My boss was not happy with me at all. It seems I was having a negative impact on the company's workforce. The people I trained left the company for better-paying positions somewhere else. It wasn't that we didn't have jobs for them. It was just that this particular company had a very narrow view of who should fill those spots. Shame on them for thinking so little of employees already on their payroll.

When you're first considering an interoffice job change, be honest with yourself. If you've had any problems in your current position, such as tardiness, reprimands, verbal or written warnings, or issues with coworkers, don't go for the job unless it's halfway across the office. Even then, don't be surprised if you're not the candidate picked to fill an open position. I've seen plenty of people who were the only candidate to apply for a job but didn't get it solely because they were some other department's problem child.

There is one warning you should heed when multiple applicants within the corporation are applying for a job. Sometimes supervisors like to have the candidates do all the work in the interview process, so they'll pit you against each other during your separate interviews. I'm not sure if this is a legitimate business practice, laziness, or cruelty, but it happens occasionally, and you need to be warned. A supervisor or manager will ask you why you think you'd be a great candidate for the job and what your strengths and weaknesses are, and this is a normal enough question. But sometimes she'll ask you your opinion about another candidate. And a manager may ask you questions about your current department or immediate supervisor. Be extremely careful about what you say. Sure, you could take this opportunity to malign a coworker, digging up all her little office secrets and baring them to the light of day. But something like this doesn't make them look half as bad as it makes you appear. Just take a moment to phrase the truth as positively as you can. If you think a coworker is slow, please don't blurt it out. Instead say, "Susan has a great disposition for the job, but she might need to take a typing course to improve her productivity." If a coworker goofs off a lot or is on the phone too much, say, "Christopher really knows his stuff, but he seems a little distracted lately. His work may be suffering, but I'm sure it's temporary. Maybe he'll be able to focus more on a new job." Usually the supervisor knows exactly what you're saying and admires your tact. If you're not careful, you'll appear sneaky and deceitful, neither of which is a quality associated with being the proverbial team player. If you feel this question is inappropriate, say so. Any question that makes you uncomfortable during the interview probably shouldn't have been asked.

You also have to learn how to be moderate with these small white lies so you don't inadvertently talk a coworker into a job you want for yourself. That really hurts. You can also talk someone else into a job that's just wrong in general. During an interview, while discussing the job description in minute detail, I realized it wasn't as attractive as I first thought. A friend of mine was applying for the same job, and although we tried not to let the competition get to us, it took a toll on our friendship. Once I realized the job wasn't for me, I withdrew my candidacy during the interview (in my book, that's allowed, because I had not received an offer), and I started talking about my friend. I gave her a glowing review, and she got the job. Shortly after taking it, she came to the same conclusion that I did; no one in her right mind would want a job like that one. When she found out that I had recommended her for it, she didn't know whether to be flattered or angry. She originally had been much more enthusiastic about the job than I had. How was I supposed to know she wouldn't want it either? After a few months, we were able to laugh about it, and the job did become something that my friend was actually happy with, but it remained the type of job I would never want to do.

Chapter 20

The Best Advice I Ever Got

The best, and the strangest, advice I ever received during my corporate career came in the form of a poor performance review. It was early in my career, and I was under the mistaken impression that all it took to succeed anywhere in business was hard work and determination. Hard work is physically demanding. The corporate workplace thrives on mental acuity. A worker must be able to think herself up the corporate ladder more than she needs to worry about an actual physical climb. I received a poor review because, in my supervisor's opinion, I didn't "anticipate my customers' needs." I was at a complete loss. How do you anticipate the needs of someone before she asks you for anything? And how do you know the needs of people you hardly know? Yet people do things like this every day. Mothers instinctively know when their children are in trouble or causing trouble. Policemen know when a small detail in a situation is suspicious. And we all get a sense of when something is amiss in the lives of our immediate family members and closest friends. But how do you do this with strangers? And more importantly, is the use of instinct a skill that you can develop and apply in a business context?

The task of learning to anticipate my customers' needs plagued me for months. I started observing people, closely looking for clues as to what they needed to get their jobs done more efficiently. But I didn't feel a connection to these people and had a hard time figuring them out, let alone figuring out what their needs were. I went back to my supervisor and asked her for guidance, but she could only tell me two things—first, that it was up to me to figure it out, and second, that my next review was just around the corner. And it didn't look like it would be any better than the last one.

I had a mentor at the office, a manager from another department, whom I could talk to about insurance courses, promotion opportunities, and corporate policies. Up until then I had never approached him to discuss a problem. But I didn't know where else to turn. I went to see him and explained my frustration at not being able to anticipate my customers' needs. I told him that my supervisor was asking me to do the impossible, and he told me I was wrong. I told him I was not a psychic, and he told me I didn't have to be. He asked me to take a walk around the office with him so he could prove his point.

As we walked around the office, he pointed to the underwriters and raters I knew and asked me questions about them. We rounded a corner and saw one particularly frustrated underwriter. "Do you see that guy over there, the one rubbing his forehead and squinting?" He was pointing to a young underwriter who had recently started working at the company. "Do you know what's wrong with him?"

And actually, I did. He was new at the company. Senior underwriters were taking advantage of him and giving him the worst accounts to work on, accounts that everyone else in the department considered the stuff of nightmares. The underwriting assistants didn't know him and had no respect for him. His work was being ignored. And on top of everything else, he was having problems with his in-laws.

My mentor looked at me and asked, "So what do you think he really needs right now, this very minute in time?"

I thought about it and said that I could offer to stay late and help him with his work. I wasn't assigned to him as an assistant, but that didn't preclude me from helping him.

What my mentor said next really surprised me. "Well, you could do that, and God knows he'd probably appreciate the offer. Or you could just find him some aspirin. Because right now his headache is real, and he needs relief from it more than anything else at this exact moment."

I excused myself and went around asking for aspirin. When I finally found some, I went up to the young underwriter and offered it to him. He looked at me with gratitude in his eyes. "I've been looking for this for thirty minutes. Thanks." I asked him if I could help him with his files. I told him it was different work than I usually performed, but I could learn it quickly. He thanked me but said that he had underwriting assistants, and it was their job to do the work. He excused himself, marched into his manager's office, and unburdened himself of his frustrations at the top of his lungs. He wanted to know why an underwriting assistant from another team felt compelled to offer to work on his files when his own assistants treated his work like it was radioactive. By the end of this lengthy discussion, his two clerks had reprimands in their files while I had a glowing written compliment. And all I did was to give the poor man some pain-relief medication and offer assistance.

In an office, your coworkers are as much your customers as the company's outside clients. In fact, depending on the position you hold at your company, your coworkers may be the only customers you have. Anticipating their needs is a matter of observation and thought. Sometimes the most important thing to a coworker in the office is not the work. We're human, and things happen. Anticipating your customers' needs puts you in a proactive position. You're not only trying to handle existing problems but prevent or diminish future ones. Start by understanding that sometimes your customer needs you to recognize that she's a human being first and an underwriter, accountant, auditor, IT tech, business analyst, claims adjuster, loss control representative, or manager second. A stressed-out colleague can't function well. Offer her some tea, or lend her a concerned ear. Tell her to take a break, and go with her outside for some fresh air and friendly conversation. Listen to what the problem really is, and offer advice when you can and support when you can't. And then take her back up to the office, and try to get her focused on her job again.

If the problem is work related, think before you offer to do anything. The young underwriter I offered to help was right. There were two people in the office being paid to help him with his accounts, and they were collecting money on a biweekly basis without doing the work. Unless I wanted their jobs, which I did not, I should never have offered to do their work. Be mindful of who really benefits from the favors you perform.

But getting back to the work problem, the trick to anticipating your customers' needs is to know your job better than you need to. If your job is to put policies together, and there are constantly problems with forms, you should be the first person trying to find a solution or work-around. A work-around is a method of performing a task outside the normal and established system. It's usually frowned upon, because if you find a way to jury-rig a faulty system, problems tend to stay problems. For instance, if you find a work-around for a computer glitch, the work gets done, but the computer program you're using stays broken or faulty. But while work-arounds are discouraged, so are missed deadlines. The first time you see a problem at any phase of your work flow, you should make it your mission to find the solution. Even if you don't, it will be noted by your supervisor that you're at least trying.

At some point after you've become good at anticipating your customers' needs, it will seem to some people that you're clairvoyant, and it may feel as if you are. But what's happened is that you've managed to retrain your brain to focus on the little details you would normally let slip by. You can tell from a person's facial expression or body language whether they're having a good day or not. Sadly, while we see these clues every day, we fail to care about them, because we're most often preoccupied with our own concerns. In order to accurately anticipate your customers' needs, you don't have to work harder or volunteer to do anything extra in the office. You just have to approach your day with an open mind. Look for the clues that people are literally throwing at you and interpret these signs in a logical way. Think before you act or react. And if worse comes to worse, keep a stash of candy bars in your desk. Chocolate does wonders in most corporate offices.

Chapter 21

Education

At some point you may choose to continue your education in order to make yourself a better candidate for the jobs you want to get. This does not necessarily mean that you need to run to get into college, but don't rule it out as an option in the foreseeable future. What it means is that you'll need to shop around and look for the most cost-effective educational options you can find. There are usually industry courses that you can take to earn certificates or gain skills that employers like, and the best news is that the company you work for will likely pay for these types of classes with no strings attached. That's because these courses are short, immediately effective, and relatively cheap when compared to the cost of college-level courses. However, the more specialized the training courses (i.e., chartered property and casualty underwriter courses for commercial underwriters, specific computer language courses, and management-level training courses), the more costly the class.

Even before you go this route, there are some free options you should take advantage of. If you didn't pick up some new skills before you applied to work at your company (as mentioned earlier), now would be a good time to do so. Free up a little time, and watch some YouTube videos on how to create Excel spreadsheets or mail merges or use Microsoft Outlook. You could even learn beginning accounting and bookkeeping tips. You'd be surprised at what information people put out there for you to freely use. Take advantage of it.

If you're more hands-on but still need to do things in your own time and at your own pace, there's a great series of books that will help you learn the ins and outs of the Microsoft Office Suite programs. The series is called the Shelly Cashman series, and it's written by Gary B. Shelly, Thomas J. Cashman, and a number of other contributing authors. The best thing about these books is that many of them can be borrowed from the public library.

I took a variety of basic and intermediate online Word and Excel classes, but I learned far more about these Microsoft programs through a class called Computers and Society that I took at Northeastern Illinois University's El Centro campus. The course was an entry-level computer class and taught the basics of Word, Excel, PowerPoint, and Access. Access gave me the most trouble, but I was still able to learn it effectively with the Shelly Cashman Series books that were used to teach this college course. And I particularly liked Microsoft *Office Excel 2007: Comprehensive Concepts and Techniques, Microsoft Office Word 2007:*

Comprehensive Concepts and Techniques and *Discovering Computers: Fundamentals.* These books not only teach you the business applications of these programs but also show you how to make flyers and calendars, do your own bookkeeping, etc. If you want to add these books to your library, most are available on Amazon.com in paperback and for Kindle.

Chapter 22

On Going to College

Harold Washington College, Chicago, IL • M. E. Jones

I hope this book has not given you the impression that I'm in any way against college. In fact, in December 2012, I graduated from Northeastern Illinois University with a BA after earning an associate's degree through the City Colleges of Chicago educational system. And at some point in the near future I plan to pursue a master's degree. But everything I've accomplished in the insurance field was done with only a high school education. This book is written for anyone interested in getting a corporate job, but its focus has been on those of you who don't yet hold degrees. You still can get a job at a good firm if you know how to do it. And once you get in, if you decide to continue your education, that's a great idea. But this section is devoted to the readers out there who are already convinced that the only way to get better job opportunities is by going to college to get a better education. If this sounds like you, read on.

Some companies provide educational benefits as part of their generous benefits packages, but before you jump for what seems like a sweet deal, look a little bit closer. Businesses will only pay for you to go to those classes that are of benefit to them, and they have a very narrow view of what is considered beneficial. Many companies could profit from sending their employees to basic college-level English 101 classes. If you're planning to become a business manager, a computer programming wizard, a human resources manager, or a business accountant, the offer of company sponsored tuition will work for you. But if you're cut from a different cloth, like me, then you may want to major in something completely unrelated. Perhaps a degree in music, cinematography, environmental studies, or culinary arts is more your speed. And even though you work in a business field, there's nothing wrong with these aspirations. Will this kind of education hinder your promotability? Not necessarily. In fact, choosing a nontraditional degree (in this case, anything not business related) may be the best decision you can make for your career.

By now, you may have heard the tired cliché, "Think outside the box." If you haven't, and you don't know what it means, it boils down to willfully being creative and thinking in revolutionary ways, which is pretty much what any employee who cares about her job does anyway. Any employer who can't see the value of hiring an employee in possession of a non-business degree is surprisingly shortsighted. Business majors are great at business, but they don't necessarily understand the average person who makes up the bulk of a company's customer base. There are a variety of degree programs that are non-business orientated and that lend themselves nicely to a corporate environment.

Take psychology for example. A psych major makes a great marketer. They understand people's behavior and in some cases can manipulate that behavior and use it to influence sales. Business majors can predict trends from a numbers standpoint; psychology majors use emotions as a barometer for business success, and they know that messages aimed at triggering strong emotions like love or fear, are powerful consumer motivators.

Sociology is another great degree to have in a business environment. Sociologists have more than one view of the world and everything that happens in it. They understand people, infrastructures, and economic sectors. They study people in groups and have a great understanding of historical and societal events that have an impact on the business sector.

Those of you who are planning on becoming English majors should know that most corporations would be lucky to get you as an employee. Many companies need technical writers, public speakers, presentation designers, communications experts, public relations personnel, and trainers. You're perfect for these jobs and more. Time permitting, you could also offer to take over the company newsletter, manage the company's website, or start a company blog if this is the kind of work you would like to perform.

Anyone majoring in criminal justice could possibly start out as a claims adjuster, a loss control service representative, or an appraiser and then eventually move to a claims fraud unit. Fraud analysis is one of the most interesting functions at an insurance company, and it's very important to have competent people investigating suspicious insurance activities. Researching suspicious claims reports takes a lot of time, but thwarting insurance cheats is a very rewarding occupation.

I'm a geographer. I've learned to use mapping programs to create maps with business applications. I can take a client list, tweak it, run it through a geographical information systems program, and map a company's client base. Such a map will show the density of a company's customers as well as areas where a company's products are purchased minimally. The same information can be used to map the distribution of specific products, the spread of damages due to natural disasters, and claims reported for specific losses such as mold damage or employee theft. I can also create area maps of the points of interest, restaurants, and hotels in Chicago and other major cities. These make great handouts for visiting dignitaries.

No, having a nontraditional degree will not stop you from being successful in a business setting. But what *will* dampen your chances of success faster than anything else is getting an education in a track you don't like or have little interest in. Majoring in business when your heart's not in it is the fastest way to become a corporate burnout and a failure. So if you decide that college is for you, choose your path based on what you really want to learn and not on what you think an education can do for you. Don't worry about second-guessing your choice of major at a later date in your life. If you're honest with yourself about the things you're passionate about, when you go back to school you'll be able to make the right educational choices. There may come a day when you think you should have taken a different path, but, right or wrong, at least you did it your way.

If you decide to become a business major, and your company has an educational benefits package, review it twice before you sign anything. Then review it again. Accepting this type of offer is like making a deal with the devil. If you don't think signing in blood is involved, just read the fine print. In exchange for educational reimbursement, most companies require you to keep your grades up (at least a B or C average), and some require you to agree to continue working for them for an additional five years after you graduate. This all sounds reasonable, but what happens if you quit, get fired, or are laid off? I once saw a woman go into shock when her employer handed her the bill for the outstanding balance of her college education at her exit interview. Her eyes rolled back in her head when she realized just how much money she owed. I don't believe they were willing to set up a modest repayment plan either. I'm not sure how they go about collecting the money they're owed, but I think wage garnishments are not out of the question.

There are four ways to avoid the sticker shock of your corporation's educational benefit package. The first way is to find a company that only has one stipulation on paying for your education—you must pass the class. There are very few such companies out there, and the only way you can find them is to call the companies you're interested in working for and ask their HR departments to explain those benefits to you. The second way is to take the package and pray you last at the company five years after you graduate. Most people do, so this is not farfetched. The third way is to save as much money over the years as you can in order to have some cash on hand to repay the debt in a pinch. The cool thing about this method is that if you survive at the company for the full five years, you don't have to repay the debt, and you eventually have thousands of dollars to play with any way you want. The last way is to bypass the company assistance altogether and pay for your education yourself.

This is the method I had help choosing. I got into an argument with my supervisor about what is and is not business related. The company would pay for my education only if I majored in business, something

I knew I didn't want to do. I countered that, while majoring in business, I would be required to take the same prerequisite classes (Math 101, English 101, Speech 100, and a host of others) as in any other major. Why couldn't the company pay for those classes, and let me pick up the tab for the other ones? Why indeed? Because corporations don't care if their employees are happy; they just want them to be profitable and productive. I ended up paying for my own education. I went to Wright College and earned an associate's degree. When my supervisor realized that I was learning advanced methods of using the Microsoft Office Suite, she wanted me to use my new skills to create quarterly reports, training manuals, PowerPoint presentations, and informational packets for clients. But I refused for several reasons, the two most important being that I wasn't being offered extra compensation to do so, and since the company I worked for had refused to contribute financially to my education, they shouldn't reap any benefits from said education. I brought in a college catalog and told her I had circled the classes she could take if she needed to work on her own computer skills. She wasn't happy with my sense of humor, but had to admit that I had a point. Many managers at that company felt that the educational benefits the company provided were limited and that the company should consider providing educational assistance to anyone seeking a degree of any type.

I want to take a moment to give a shout-out to all the community colleges across the United States. People have a tendency to consider the educational value of community colleges to be limited, but that's only because they haven't attended one. There's a misconception that you go to a community college when you want to skate through school getting "easy A's." At Wilbur Wright College in Chicago, they don't give you any easy grades. They don't give you anything. You have to work very hard to keep up your GPA. The same hard work required at a traditional four-year institution is required at community colleges. The amount of reading required at Wilbur Wright College was nothing compared to the amount of writing required, and that was nothing compared to the amount of thought required for each and every assignment I received. I was a night student, and every day for the first year and a half, I wondered why I was putting myself through this experience. About a semester away from graduation, I finally saw light at the end of a very long tunnel. Although every day had been a challenge, it went by more quickly than I ever imagined it would. I urge anyone thinking about attending classes at a community college—even just one—to go for it. It's the greatest value for the price you'll ever find. If you can't get financial assistance, attending classes through a community college is the most economical way to continue your education.

Chapter 23

A Five-Year Investment

I want to make a very important point here: unless you absolutely love your job, once you've been in a position for five years, either go for a promotion or get out of the company. Those who are managing to get annual pay increases from their employers do not understand how longevity on the job can hurt them financially. That's because most companies have a rule that employees are not allowed to talk to each other about pay grades or salaries and increases. This is understandable. The topic of salaries can be as volatile as conversations about religion, politics, and gun control. People believe in entitlements. They think everyone should get paid the same amount. Most people think they're actually worth a little more than the people around them. But the longer you sit in a job, even with periodic raises, the less you'll make over time compared to the fresh employees coming in the door today. There are people out there who have been in the same non-managerial positions for ten years or more and who have no idea that their salaries are comparable to those of the new employees just coming into the office. And in many cases, they're secretly making far less money than those same new employees. Sadly, there's little chance that they'll ever figure it out.

A variety of factors make up your salary. The first is the industry standards that dictate what an employee in the Midwest is paid as compared to one in California or one in New York. Work experience counts to some degree, but if you don't gain new skills, over time the new people coming in can and will catch up with, or exceed, your skill level. From your employer's point of view, your salary is part of their overhead, the never-ending expense of doing business. I've had only one employer who worried that they were not paying me enough money. They couldn't pay me any more cash, but they came up with unique ways to compensate me for my time. That was one employer out of ten. The other nine were the normal employers, trying to figure out how to give me just enough money to keep me working for them while they were trying to figure out where to find the money needed to get new talent to come through their doors. The term *new talent* doesn't just apply to inexperienced workers but to seasoned employees who will be new to the company. Although inexperienced workers generally come into a company at lower pay grades than that company's long-term employees, it's not unusual for some new employees to get offers for salaries that are significantly higher. This is because new employees are often seen as a source of innovation, and companies are willing to pay people a little extra, if their bosses see potential in them. Seasoned employees who are coming in from other companies already make what you're making, and so the offers they receive must be higher to entice them to change jobs. Every dime they get comes from somewhere. If a company is doing well, that "somewhere" is usually from their investments. If a company is not doing very well, "somewhere" usually involves restructuring and downsizing. If a company is doing poorly, "somewhere" means wage freezes and reduction in benefits. And in all three scenarios, "somewhere" is located right around *your* pocket.

It's time for a math break. You start working for a company making ten dollars an hour as a file clerk. You get a 4 percent increase annually (if you're lucky). Two years later you wouldn't even make a dollar more an hour. If you stay in the department for five years, your new annual salary would be $24,336—roughly $1.70 an hour more than the starting wage you earned five years ago. Now let's say you were ready to leave the company and become a records clerk somewhere else. Are you going to make that move for $11.70 an hour? No, because it wouldn't make sense to do that. You'd be giving up some benefits at this point, like stock options and being vested in your 401K, maybe even a small pension, if they still exist. You'd have a strict probationary period as your new company tries to determine whether they really want to keep you or not. Even though you have experience, you'd have to go through training again to learn your new employer's systems and work flows. And you'd have to break in new coworkers and get your bearings at this new place. How much money is it going to take for you to start over again? There's a good chance that $11.70 an hour is now the industry standard for fresh employees with no skills. Maybe it's even less than the industry standard. You have five years' worth of skills. It wouldn't be unreasonable to expect an increase of between three thousand and five thousand dollars, depending on the financial standing of the new company you're trying to join.

If we take the low end, you'd ask for $27,336. I like to go a little high and let them come back with a lower offer. What I'd really want is $27,500, so I'd ask for $28,200. Remember, you were only making $24,336, so if they offer twenty-seven thousand dollars flat, even though it's less than three thousand dollars more than your last job, take it! You'd be making $12.98 an hour, which is still better than $11.70 an hour. But honestly, I think you can do better. Remember that this example started by using the low end of what you could expect in the way of a salary increase just by changing jobs. In reality, you should always aim for the high end.

If you get an offer that isn't exactly what you want, you have three choices. You can reject it, which I would do only if I found something else wrong with the company, like a high turnover of employees, recent layoffs, office closures, no signs of promotion opportunities, or the other benefits don't stack up to what I already have. You can use this offer to try to get more money out of your current employer, but I wouldn't do this, because managers and business owners have long memories, and this isn't how they think loyal employees should behave. Remember, few bosses will ever believe they're underpaying you. If you try to leverage another offer against your current salary, they will lose trust in you and expect you to do this again in the near future whenever you want more cash. Unless they really like you or can't do without you and your skill set, if they keep you around, it won't be for long. They'll replace you as soon as a better candidate comes along. Your last choice is to take the offer and make the best of it. This is the choice I would pick. Once you're in a new company, you can usually find benefits somewhere that will make up for not getting every cent you wanted in your salary. And sometimes, depending on the financial state of the company, you can earn bonuses outside your normal increases that will drive your annual income up higher than you ever thought you could get it to go.

Chapter 24

Be Careful What You Wish For

As you go after promotions or change jobs, be careful to fully investigate each opportunity that comes along before you decide to pursue it. Things often appear better on the surface than they actually are. Money is tempting, but don't let it cause you to make some of the mistakes I've made.

After several years of working at American Country Insurance Company as an underwriting assistant, I was offered the opportunity to do a massive amount of overtime to tackle a huge backlog of work. I was able to save ten thousand dollars in a period of seven months. I was also due for an increase in pay. I was very disappointed when my usually hefty increase amounted to only a 3 percent cost-of-living raise. I wanted more. I discussed this with my manager. I was told that I had capped what I could get in the way of an annual increase as an underwriting assistant. The only way to get the kind of money I wanted was to take a promotion to underwriter. We haggled about compensation. I asked for a ten-thousand-dollar increase, then a seven-thousand-dollar increase, and I settled for five thousand.

I thought everything was great until that next paycheck. I was underwhelmed by what I saw as a net figure. I inadvertently had put myself into a higher tax bracket. My check was barely different from the one I received as an assistant. In fact, I think my paycheck may have even decreased. But the big change was that I no longer qualified for overtime pay. I was still expected to work the extra hours and more. I had accepted a five-thousand-dollar increase and would end up making around five thousand dollars less every year. True, the overtime was not guaranteed, but for the next three years, I kept mental notes of how much money I was losing as a salaried employee, and it made me cry.

But the horror didn't stop there. There were many other perks I'd taken for granted over the years that I also no longer qualified for: games at Christmas parties where the participants won cash and prizes, employee-of-the-month competitions, drawings for spare sporting-event tickets, and other such incentives were strictly for employees making an hourly wage. I could kiss all of those perks good-bye.

Several years later my department lost its largest client. Our work was consolidated within another department, and there were too many underwriters for the work that remained. I was laterally promoted to a business analyst. Traditionally a business analyst is a person who looks at a company's organizational structure and work flows, analyzes instances of redundancies, and makes recommendations to trim the fat and become more profitable. At insurance companies the term *business analyst* is being used as a title for any job that lacks a defined direction or doesn't fit under any other title. As a business analyst for American Country, I tested their new policy issuance system to determine if it worked properly. It was a repetitive job that needed to be done. I just wish they could have found someone else to do it. When my boss took me away from the underwriting department, the skills that I had worked so hard to develop during my career quickly atrophied. I was good at being their version of a business analyst, but when a layoff occurred two years later, I found out just how useless that title and those skills really were. I applied for jobs as a business analyst at several other companies, but most required computer programming skills I didn't have. After six months, I removed *business analyst* from my résumé, and I took a job several steps backward in order to gain employment. My quest to the top of the corporate ladder began anew.

Conclusion

Sounds like a lot of work, doesn't it? Well, it is. Whether you're content to be a mail room clerk your entire life or you want to become the CEO of your own company one day, you need to put as much effort as possible into getting, keeping, and protecting the job you want in your chosen career path. At Northeastern Illinois University, I was introduced to the concept of frontloading coursework by one of my instructors, Professor Charles Schmidt. Professor Schmidt explained to all of his students that frontloading involved putting all the hard work into a project at the beginning of it so that by the time you got to the end of it, your earlier momentum made the task easier to complete when you started to run out of steam. I realized that I'd been applying this technique to my job opportunities as well. I accepted a job as a records clerk and frontloaded the experience by reading everything that came across my desk, in depth. When I moved to the mail and supply department, I did the same thing, but I added the practice of looking out for job opportunities wherever I could find them. While in the mail and supply department, I frontloaded my next career move as I began to seek training from friends who already had the next job I wanted. And this strategy continues today. I just finished a ninety-day probationary period on a new job, and on the ninetieth day, I jumped to take advantage of their no-strings-attached educational programs. Each passed class is tied into a bonus program. There are ten classes involved in getting a chartered-property-and-casualty-underwriter designation, and I plan to get as many of those classes under my belt as I possibly can through this corporation.

Corporate America is a rough place to work, but that should not discourage anyone from experiencing the climb to the top. Some people will make it, and others won't. But everyone should try it at least once in his or her life. I believe in experiencing everything you can in life. A career in a corporate environment is unlike anything else in the world. Sometimes the things that happen at corporations defy logic and reality, especially when some of the most profitable companies feel the need to operate with skeleton crews, or there are wage freezes for everyone except management personnel, or seasoned employees lose opportunities to their coworkers' untrained children. But the benefits offered by corporations in the way of monetary compensation and professional and educational opportunities make it all worth it. The stress of these jobs is high, but the rewards that come with being a successful corporate worker are high as well.

Most employers are now looking for employees who have college educations, but if you don't have one yet, you can still make your way into a corporate job if you first gain some skills, gather information about the company you want to work for, and practice selling yourself to your prospective employer, all in advance of your first interview. Remember that a college education doesn't automatically mean that someone is a computer-savvy, business-literate, people person. In business today, life experience counts too. Make yourself as presentable on paper and in person as you can, and you'll be able to compete along with everyone else. College graduates only have the upper hand in an interview when an employer makes having a degree a requirement for getting the job. The rest of the time, the most personable person or the biggest BSer will get the job, regardless of educational background. This is not meant to downplay the value of having a college degree in today's job market. I just believe there's something more important to have in your possession as you begin looking for a corporate job—self-confidence.

One of my greatest assets is a high level of self-confidence, and if you want to do well in business, you need to develop yours as much as you possibly can. If you have a fear of public speaking, consider joining a local chapter of Toastmasters International, a nonprofit organization that helps people develop awesome public speaking skills. If you doubt your ideas or think that they can't be as good as someone else's, get over that negative thinking. Everyone has a point of view and yours has just as much merit as the next person's. Learn to speak up for yourself, your ideas, and the things you believe in. If you're unsure of yourself because you don't think your experiences and educational level are equal to the tasks involved in performing a corporate job satisfactorily, slap yourself and do something about it. Take a class, start studying skills at the library through books, asked a professional you know for help. Fight for your right to get a shot at an office job. If you know you have the ability to learn, work hard, and grow as an employee, that's fifty percent of the qualities you need to feel confident about yourself as a person. If you have any doubts about your abilities, write them down on a piece of paper, and either work through these anxieties or set that page on fire. Everyone starts out skittish in the workforce. But in order to get an employer to believe in you enough to give you a job in the first place, you have to believe in yourself. You may not get the first job you go after or the second or the third, but you shouldn't let that discourage you from trying to find another, better opportunity. Eventually you'll find a job, and if you've paid any attention to what I've been trying to tell you in this book, it'll be the perfect fit for you.

Self-confidence is a marvelous tool, and the first step to obtaining it is to just stand up with your chin up high and your eyes wide open. Get up, find a job you want to try, and go for it with gusto.

One thing you really need to know about advancement within a corporation is that in most cases it's not accomplished in a straight line but in more of a zigzag pattern. Advancement can be accomplished in a more forward manner through which you get a job and slowly advance within a department and possibly make it to a managerial position you can eventually retire from. But I think my way is a lot more lucrative and entertaining. Plus, in our current economy, it's best to have as many viable skills as you possibly can.

In my insurance career, I went from being a records clerk to a records work leader to a mail clerk to a mail and supply specialist to a rater/coder/keyer to a commercial lines rater to an underwriting assistant to a commercial service representative to an underwriter to a business analyst and then back to an underwriting assistant. I'm now aiming for a chartered property casualty underwriter designation, but where I go from here is really anyone's guess.

I have a little less than twenty years left in this industry, and I plan to make every day count. Pursuing insurance classes will keep me busy for the next two years, but after that—well, I see new, possibly managerial tasks in my future. And teaching. My recent experience at college taught me that I have a fondness for imparting wisdom to others. That's a big reason why I wrote this book.

I hope that somewhere out there a person who's stuck in a dead-end job picks up this book and is able to use the stories and suggestions in it to get her foot in the door at a large, possibly international corporation. Getting in is the hardest part. And once you get in, keep a copy of this book handy and revisit it from time to time. Don't just use it as a guide. Use it as a measuring stick against your own experiences, and see how they compare with mine. Then once you establish yourself in your field, put it down and write your own stories.

Employment at corporations, even in entry-level jobs, is not for everyone. In the lowest positions, you're often treated like dirt, even when you do everything asked of you and more. But instead of letting it upset you, use it as motivation to climb up the corporate ladder as quickly as possible. What could be more satisfying on the job than advancing above a boss who's tormented you for years or pushing him or her into considering an early retirement?

Here are some final thoughts for you. Once you start climbing that corporate ladder, don't look down. Try to get to the top cleanly, but if you cause casualties on the way up, just remember that, sadly, it's better them than you. You can't be everyone's friend no matter how much you want to be. Remember that every skill you pick up today, no matter how insignificant it seems, will be an asset on your résumé tomorrow. And while you're an ambitious person, you should know that you too are running around the office with a big old target on you back. Watch out! You're not the only one running for the summit.